HOW
TO PRAY
IN A
CRISIS

HOW TO PRAY IN A CRISIS

A 4-Step Guide to Renewal

Daniel Henderson

MOODY PUBLISHERS
CHICAGO

Portions of this book are adapted from Daniel Henderson's books *Old Paths, New Power: Awakening Your Church through Prayer and the Ministry of the Word* (Chicago: Moody Publishers, 2016); *Transforming Prayer: How Everything Changes When You Seek God's Face* (Bloomington, MN: Bethany House Publishers, 2011); and *Transforming Presence: How the Holy Spirit Changes Everything from the Inside-Out* (Chicago: Moody Publishers, 2018).

Scripture quotations, unless otherwise indicated, are from The Holy Bible, English Standard Version® (ESV®), copyright © 2001 by Crossway, a publishing ministry of Good News Publishers. Used by permission. All rights reserved.

Scripture quotations marked KJV are taken from the King James Version.

Scripture quotations marked NASB are taken from the New American Standard Bible® (NASB), Copyright © 1960, 1962, 1963, 1968, 1971, 1972, 1973, 1975, 1977, 1995 by The Lockman Foundation. Used by permission. www.Lockman.org

Scripture quotations marked NIV are taken from the Holy Bible, New International Version®, NIV®. Copyright © 1973, 1978, 1984, 2011 by Biblica, Inc.™ Used by permission of Zondervan. All rights reserved worldwide. www.zondervan.com The "NIV" and "New International Version" are trademarks registered in the United States Patent and Trademark Office by Biblica, Inc.™

Scripture marked NKJV taken from the New King James Version®. Copyright © 1982 by Thomas Nelson. Used by permission. All rights reserved.

Scripture quotations marked AMPC are taken from the Amplified® Bible (AMPC), Copyright © 1954, 1958, 1962, 1964, 1965, 1987 by The Lockman Foundation. Used by permission. www.Lockman.org

All emphasis in Scripture has been added.

Edited by Connor Sterchi
Interior Design: Erik M. Peterson
Cover Design: Kaylee Lockenour

Library of Congress Control Number: 2020940743

ISBN: 978-0-8024-2359-7

Originally delivered by fleets of horse-drawn wagons, the affordable paperbacks from D. L. Moody's publishing house resourced the church and served everyday people. Now, after more than 125 years of publishing and ministry, Moody Publishers' mission remains the same—even if our delivery systems have changed a bit. For more information on other books (and resources) created from a biblical perspective, go to www.moodypublishers.com or write to:

Moody Publishers
820 N. LaSalle Boulevard
Chicago, IL 60610

1 3 5 7 9 10 8 6 4 2

Printed in the United States of America

CONTENTS

FOREWORD

Trials in my life and ministry have taught me an important lesson: hard is hard; hard is not bad. Difficult times bring struggles and questions. Pain makes way for lament—a prayer language to navigate between the poles of a hard life and God's sovereignty.

After my wife and I endured the heart-breaking loss of a stillborn daughter, lament became a new grace in my life. I discovered that prayers of lament helped me through struggle and pain. Prayer, especially lament, is a humble turning to God *in* the crisis for a believer living *through* crisis.

Crisis reorients our hearts toward what is true. But for that to happen, we must to turn to prayer. The silence must end. Frustration and discouragement might tempt us to stop talking to God. But He is able to turn our honest questions into confident trust in our hardest times.

We cannot stop making this turn toward trust. We learn to live in the tension of pain beyond belief and divine sovereignty beyond comprehension by faith. Trust will always lead us to a place of praise. We can actually learn to sing and worship when crisis comes our way.

What we *learn* must then become what we *live*. This is where *How to Pray in a Crisis* by my friend Daniel Henderson comes in. No one has taught me more about the practice of prayer. Daniel is the rare combination of theologian and practitioner. He's studied prayer while leading people in prayer. And that experience is why he's the perfect person to write a book about praying in a crisis. He's done it. Lived it. Many times.

This book guides you into the fullness of what God wants to teach you in, through, and beyond your crisis. A new lifestyle of biblical conviction and rich community awaits you. A fresh discovery of competency in prayer can be yours. You will be invited to vital participation in a hopeful and supernatural advancement of the gospel into our crisis-plagued world.

The promise for Christians in crisis is as glorious as it is deep. The cross shows us that God has already proven Himself to be for us, not against us, no matter what we face. Jesus bought the right to make everything right:

> As it is written, "For your sake we are being killed all the day long; we are regarded as sheep to be slaughtered." No, in all these things we are more than conquerors through him who loved us. For I am sure that neither death nor life, nor angels nor rulers, nor things present nor things to come, nor powers, nor height nor depth, nor anything else in all creation, will be able to separate us from the love of God in Christ Jesus our Lord. (Rom. 8:36–39)

During my deepest season of pain, John Piper exhorted me, "Keep trusting the one who keeps you trusting." God initiates the call to seek Him through our prayers of confident trust. He also empowers and equips us to enjoy Him in the wonder of His worthiness.

My prayer is that this book will guide you to a lifestyle of new beginnings in your communion with God and your influence for Him. As people all around you struggle to cope with crisis, the hope within you can be a light in the darkness of a broken world.

MARK VROEGOP
Lead Pastor, College Park Church
Author, *Dark Clouds, Deep Mercy: Discovering the Grace of Lament*

THE CROSSROADS OF YOUR CRISIS

If you are in a crisis of any kind right now, God has brought you to a divinely orchestrated crossroads. The higher path calls you to renewed trust and transformation. The lower one allures you to hide in the cocooned space of comfort, complacency, and self-protection.

In His goodness, God sovereignly superintends all crises, desiring to use them for good. He is not absent in our consternation, pain, and uncertainty. Rather than obsess with *why* the crisis happened, we are wise to inquire of the Lord as to *what* we are supposed to learn and *how* we can truly grow when it is all said and done.

Many notable politicians and business leaders have

referenced the Chinese word for "crisis" as a combination of two characters representing "danger" and "opportunity." While this is actually a slight mistranslation of the Chinese language, a more exact meaning of the Chinese word is "a point where things happen, change."[1] One Chinese proverb says "a crisis is an opportunity riding a dangerous wind." The principle remains that any crisis, while often precarious, presents an invitation to necessary and hopeful growth.

Prayer is truly our resource for finding comfort and relief in anxious times (see Phil. 4:6–7). Throughout the Bible, people in trouble cried out to the Lord for assurance, relief, and direction. We learn to pray with renewed dependence, even desperation, in a season of crisis. We also have the opportunity to learn to pray *beyond* the crisis in a new lifestyle of intimacy with the Lord that strengthens us with daily grace and resets our hearts toward His purpose for our lives on this earth.

This book is primarily a game plan for a deeper lifestyle of relationship with Christ and a call to participate in a powerful, potential work of genuine personal renewal and an ongoing work of vital participation in God's design for our short appearance on this earth. We will focus on prayer that is not just therapeutic but transformational. I believe that most people, at a deep level, want to be a vital part of a divine moment when supernatural things happen and life as we know it permanently changes for the sake of the gospel.

CRISIS IS ALWAYS CLARIFYING

On the one hand, a crisis helps to shape us into what we can become, but crisis also reveals what we, in reality, already are. Our instinctive reactions to a crisis often pull back the covers on our concealed insecurities, doubts, and vulnerable places in our faith. I believe that, while the challenges of life develop character, the crises of life define it.

The COVID-19 pandemic exposed already-existing vulnerabilities in many companies. The *Wall Street Journal*, writing about the bankruptcy of the 102-year-old car rental company, Hertz, noted, "The coronavirus has been the proverbial tide going out, exposing who's swimming naked."[2] The

ON THE ONE HAND, A CRISIS HELPS TO SHAPE US INTO WHAT WE CAN BECOME, BUT CRISIS ALSO REVEALS WHAT WE, IN REALITY, ALREADY ARE.

same has inevitably been true regarding the commitment of many "Christians." They feel like they are swimming in the faith without proper clothing.

In times like these we may need to reset our hearts to seek God in the storm. We can readjust our passions toward His purposes. We can recommit ourselves to His gospel plans in our seasons of deep uncertainty. As we do, we can trust that He will reshape us into more faithful and fruitful Christ-followers on the other side of any crisis.

CRISIS CAN REINFORCE CONVICTION

Christ often strips away the superficial, the tangential, the unreliable—and drives us to the things that matter most. The new convictions that arise from our seasons of crisis are often life-changing and lasting.

CRISIS AMPLIFIES COMMUNITY

As the shelter-in-place restrictions of COVID-19 began to lift, social media lit up with excitement as countless posts spoke volumes about the rightful Christian longing for community. But this need for fellowship is more than cookies, coffee, and a Styrofoam cup while standing around in the lobby chatting about sports scores. The true hunger of a redeemed soul is for biblical, deep, and authentic sense of connection, support, and mutual encouragement known and cherished only by those who belong to the body of Christ.

I propose that this community is most powerfully experienced in the context of extraordinary prayer as taught and modeled in the New Testament. This kind of prayer has historically been intricately linked to seasons of spiritual awakening, especially in times of crisis. Now is a crucial time for a fresh clarification and call to biblical community rooted in united, authentic connection with God.

CRISIS CAN SPARK COMPETENCY

Crisis forces us out of the comfort zone into the clarification zone, out of lethargy to a new opportunity for learning. We cannot coast during a crisis. We are wise to recommit to the rhythms that ultimately stabilize and satisfy.

It is my hope that *How to Pray in a Crisis* will encourage you to return to the biblical patterns of communion with God that produce lasting transformation. You will be equipped to pray more effectively but also to lead your family, your small group, even your church in experiences of life-giving prayer. This is an underestimated but essential competency in the church today. Perhaps God is using your current crisis to get you on your knees. For certain, He wants to use this crisis to keep you on your knees with an accelerated hunger for Him.

This refining and renewing grace of our Lord can help dads step up to lead their families. Moms can tune in more intentionally to the unique needs of their children. Pastors can find new discernment to distinguish between traditional rituals and life-changing realities.

This book concludes with a specific and strategic call to action. If we can all join together for such a time as this, with a resolve to serve faithfully as agents of true renewal —in the home, church, workplace, and neighborhood— the fruit of our united commitment could very well be world-changing.

EMPOWERING SCARS

Crises in our lives can often leave us with what I call "open wounds"—spiritually and emotionally. After the darkest season of my ministry, I came to a helpful realization. Our open wounds usually become tender scabs and eventually can transform into empowering scars.

The *open wound* stage is common during and shortly after a crisis. We are in deep pain. Disoriented. Angry. We prefer to hide from the world rather than face the gnawing heartache and complications of our confusion. Sometimes we question God. If people have contributed to our anguish, we battle deep resentment—even retaliation. To move forward, we must surrender our wounds to a wounded Savior who suffered for greater and holy purposes, knowing that He can pour mercy into our hurt and give us abundant grace to heal and move forward.

The *tender scab* stage follows. We begin to feel the empowerment of God's divine wisdom to see the lessons that came with tragedy. We find strength to grow in holiness and wholeness as the initial pain subsides and the road ahead glimmers with hope. But certain conversations, people, or situations "pick the scab." We see trickles of the blood from the previous crisis. Rather than regressing back to the old emotions, or even sinful reactions, this emotional prick compels us to keep moving forward, trusting in new, daily grace to become stronger and better.

The *empowering scar* eventually serves as a reminder of the redeeming power of God to use our crisis, our suffering, our questions, and our grace-empowered choices to lead us to real transformation. Scars become leading lessons that allow us to minister more powerfully and caringly to others. As Paul wrote, "From now on let no one cause me trouble, for I bear on my body the marks of Jesus" (Gal. 6:17). His suffering (we might say His history of enduring and navigating crises) were His marks of credibility. Granted, His scars were physical, but I would suggest not only physical. Scars were reminders of great grace in the journey. Great lessons gained. Expanded ministry granted.

This book is written in hopes that you have moved beyond the *open wound* stage. My prayer is that you are navigating through the *tender scab* experience as you move beyond the crisis. I pray you are realizing that God has given you an *empowering scar* or two (or ten). Perhaps now, like Paul, you are ready to join Christ in His mission with more credibility. Or with deeper conviction, greater engagement in community, a fruitful competency in prayer, and a more contagious faith in and for Jesus.

The scars that remain with us from our crises make

us more like Jesus Christ in our purposes and passions. That's why we have to pray in, and through, the crises of our lives.

CRISIS FORCES US TO CHOOSE

In the midst of any crisis we are faced with choices. We cannot just set up camp at the crossroads presented to us. We can decide to fully cooperate with the redeeming purposes of God so that we might be renewed. Conversely, we can choose to surrender to the pressures of the surrounding circumstances and remain in a rut of commonplace living. Yes, it is a shame to waste a crisis—especially for believers who, by God's grace, are fully enabled to come forth as gold after the nonessentials have been burned away by the fiery trial.

Join me as we recommit to that which God's people have always been called to do in a crisis. For the responsive, the moment can become a life-changing reset that establishes a lasting life trajectory of fulfillment and fruitfulness. For the nonresponsive, this crossroads may simply result in a temporary reprieve and gradual return to status quo after the pressure has eased.

We are familiar with the choice the Lord offered the Jewish people in view of a possible future crisis:

> "When I shut up the heavens so that there is no rain, or command the locust to devour the land, or send pestilence among my people, if my people who are called by my name humble themselves, and pray and seek my face and turn from their wicked ways, then I will hear from heaven and will forgive their sin and heal their land." (2 Chron. 7:13–14)

Yes, let us choose well. Let us pray biblically, passionately, and enduringly. Let us live victoriously long after the crisis has passed—because another one might just be looming around the corner. And, by God's grace, when it comes we will be living in strong, vital renewal.

DECIDE TO LET GOD BIRTH FRESH **CONVICTION**[1]

*At least five times the Faith
has to all appearances gone to the dogs.
In each of these five cases, it was the dog that died.*
G. K. Chesterton

*I never want to let fear of the unexpected
cause me to institutionalize lukewarmness.*
Jim Cymbala

Imagine sitting down one morning at the kitchen table. The sun streams across the room inviting you to another ordinary day. Coffee in hand, you grab your phone, glancing at your favorite news app with little anticipation except to discover more depressing stories about economic woes, international conflict, crimes of various varieties, and more political punditry. Suddenly, a riveting headline arrests your attention.

From *USA Today:*

Conversions to Christianity Multiply Exponentially, Church Leaders Cannot Explain Why.

With curiosity on high-alert, you begin a search for similar stories. Unexpectedly, the news reports leap off the screen. You can't believe what you are seeing.

From New York City:

Five Rabbis Leave their Synagogues for Christian Church after Dramatic Conversion

From Minneapolis:

Dozens of Islamic Leaders Renounce Their Faith to Join Christian Movement

From Orange Country, Calif.:
**Local Buddhist Priests Cause Stir
by Declaring that Jesus Christ Is God**

From Salt Lake City:
**Mormon Leaders to Discard Extra-Biblical
Documents in Dramatic Shift of Core Beliefs**

From New England:
Recent Surveys Show Sales of Bibles Up 200%

From *Time* magazine:
**Leading Atheists Embrace Evidence for Jesus'
Resurrection, Offer Public Apologies to Christians**

A mix of excitement and disbelief grip your core. You
have prayed for this, although not always in faith. You have
longed for this kind of breakthrough in your own church,
wondering if it would ever come. You recall that, in recent days, you have seen an unusual uptick in prayer on
social media and fresh stirrings of the Spirit among the
people in your church. But now this. It seems the prayers
of God's people over decades of desperate intercession are

now coming to fruition, redeeming opponents of the gospel and transforming communities across the landscape.

And it has come just in time. Society is on edge as racial divide is dominating the news. Various studies have pointed to a dramatic downturn in the spiritual influence of the church. The cultural indicators have screamed a thunderous warning that America is in a rapid post-Christian spiral. Believers have actually been portrayed as the obstructionists in a secular society defined by tolerance toward everything, except absolute truth. A widespread health and financial crisis has threatened all the norms of life around the world.

As you read these reports you cannot escape the thought that something truly supernatural has quietly emerged. You've heard about the Great Awakenings and their impact on society in previous centuries. Could this be the inauguration of a similar work of the Spirit? What might this mean for your family and community in the future? Could this become a wave of extraordinary grace to calm our worries over job loss and anxiety about health concerns? Is God pouring out divine unifying power to resolve racial divides in the nation? Might the Holy Spirit be working powerfully to give comfort to the lonely, peace to the uncertain soul, and new purpose to those who have simply given up? What role should you play in this rising tide of redemption?

COULD IT HAPPEN?

Could a moment like this happen in our lifetime? I would propose that it could indeed. Not only has it happened in our not-so-distant history, usually birthed in seasons of economic downturn and societal desperation, but this kind of transforming gospel impact is recorded in the New Testament.

A SUPERNATURAL HIGH POINT

I invite you to ponder with me what I believe is the greatest "revival" moment in the New Testament narrative. Transcending a difficult environment of persecution and threat, one that would soon go from tough to tougher, the early Christians form a fearless gospel community. In Acts 6:7 we read these words:

> And the word of God continued to increase, and the number of the disciples multiplied greatly in

Jerusalem, and a great many of the priests became obedient to the faith.

Read that again slowly. Absorb the incalculable impact described in this one succinct sentence. It is notable that for the first five chapters in the book of Acts, thousands were being "added" to the church in Jerusalem. In Acts 6:1, the text says they were "increasing in number." Some scholars believe the church could have had as many as 20,000 men and women as chapter 6 commences.[2] But by verse 7, it says that the number of gospel-transformed lives had "multiplied greatly." Put away the calculator. The numbers were officially off the chart. The Spirit was on the move. The gospel was going viral.

CRISIS CAN ELEVATE A BELIEVER'S FOCUS BEYOND JUST *THEIR* WORLD TO FEEL A SINCERE AND COMPELLING BURDEN FOR *THE* WORLD.

All this was occurring in a dynamic context of crisis. The young church was facing the heat of angry persecution. They were managing an internal uprising of complaint and potential division as the widow-feeding program had malfunctioned. We also know that devastating famine would soon rock and redistribute Christians in the Jerusalem congregation.

But don't miss this astounding observation: a "great many" Jewish priests were being converted. Hard-liners. Opponents of the gospel. This powerful network of religious rivals who conspired to crucify Christ was now losing a significant number from their own ranks to a transformation found in the life of the resurrected Jesus. It would be like a modern-day salvation wave that engulfs some of the most notable atheists, skeptics, celebrities, domestic terrorists, and critics of the faith. Truly amazing. Truly God. Truly possible!

A NEW CALL TO AN OLD CONVICTION

Historically, many seasons of spiritual awakening occurred in a time of crisis.[3] Why? Crisis is used by God to bring us to fresh places of humility, repentance, and essential conviction about the things that ultimately matter. Crisis can elevate a believer's focus beyond just *their* world to feel a sincere and compelling burden for *the* world. This conviction spurs a wholehearted persuasion that sets an uncompromising course of action and persistent effort.

This is the point where everything changes in our lives, families, and ministries.

Looking back on my own journey, I now know that the greatest seasons of growth occurred during the toughest of times. It may have been navigating one of numerous church crises, agonizing over a prodigal child, or trying to launch my current ministry during a huge economic downturn when our expenses far outweighed our income. We all look back and know the special grace and profound lessons of crisis, but we are ultimately wise to look around right now and know that God's school of spiritual excellence is still in session.

A CONVICTION OF RENEWED HOPE

I can't help it. Even in the hardest of days, I still wake up with a dream of another world-transforming movement of the Spirit. Looking. Longing for those headlines. Do you dream too? Could it happen again? Could it explode in our lifetime? Could unthinkable spiritual renewal supersede unprecedented societal upheaval?

Can we embrace a conviction that we each must participate in a world-changing explosion of faith even in the midst of a world-shaking epidemic of fear? Could you be used by God to see the gospel spread like wildfire and countless lives changed? Maybe your heart is feeling a compulsion, as mine has, that the "next new thing" must be "the first old thing"—especially for such a time as this. As Os Guiness noted, "The church always goes forward best by going back first."[4] Crisis offers a reset for changing the way we pray, live, and influence the world around us.

A CONVICTION ABOUT
DESPERATE DEPENDENCE

Before we look more specifically at the Acts 6 moment, I want to emphasize the broader reality of the book of Acts, which is best titled "Acts of the Holy Spirit." We will see that at the foundation of all that unfolded in this incredible history of the early days of the church, there is a conviction about prayer.

Perhaps you've seen the popular acronym PUSH (Pray Until Something Happens). I define prayer as "intimacy with God that leads to the fulfillment of His purposes." The early church was commanded by Jesus and convinced in their soul that intimacy (abiding in Chirst) would align, unite, and empower them to fulfill the Lord's purposes for their lives, individually and in community with one another.

- In the upper room, they prayed together for ten days until the coming of the Holy Spirit on the Day of Pentecost (see Luke 24:49, Acts 1:14).
- In their daily gatherings, they prayed in one accord so that Christ would be formed in them as true disciples (see Acts 2:42).
- On a daily basis, the leaders prayed, trusting to be led by the Spirit into the next unfolding chapter of life-transforming gospel ministry (see Acts 3:1).
- In Acts 6:4 the apostles uncompromisingly held to the priority of prayer, convinced that the very DNA of ministry must be marked by the power and presence of the Holy Spirit.
- Saul, after his Damascus road conversion, instinctively prayed until God brought Ananias to pray for the restoration of his sight and the launching of his ministry (Acts 9:11–12).
- The Gentile Cornelius prayed in Caesarea while Peter prayed on a rooftop until God revealed to them the

expansion of the gospel to the Gentiles (Acts 10).

- The church prayed together earnestly when Peter was in prision, until God intervened in miraculous ways according to His will (Acts 12:5).
- The second half of the book of Acts is launched as united in prayer, and the Holy Spirit spoke to them and launched them into all the world with the mission of the gospel (Acts 13:1–3).
- When beaten and locked deep in prison, Paul and Silas prayed until God revealed His delivering power to keep them on mission for the sake of His name (Acts 16:25–34).

Like our spiritual ancestors, we can discover new opportunity in every crisis if we will pray until something happens.

OUR DECLARATION OF DEPENDENCE

It may appear on my tombstone, I've said it so often: "Prayerlessness is my declaration of independence from God." Conversely, prayerfulness is my declaration of desperate dependence on God.

WHEN WE ARE CONFRONTED BY THREATENING DIFFICULTIES, WE INSTINCTIVELY SCRAMBLE TO FIND A WAY OUT. BUT GOD MAY BE CALLING US TO FIND A WAY UP.

When we are confronted by threatening difficulties, we instinctively scramble to find a way out. But God may be calling us to find a way up. He often calls us to passionately look to Him in trustful prayer, submitting to His purposes, whatever they may bring. We tend to strategize a creative way to get over the difficulty, but God is showing us the way down, in deeper humility with roots of reliance nourished in His sufficiency, come what may. John Baille prayed honestly, "When you call me to go through the dark valley, do not let me persuade myself that I know a way around."[5]

A CULTIVATED DESPERATION

A Ugandan pastor speaking at a conference hosted by my church announced, "My message to America is desperation or devastation. The choice is yours." His words are uncomfortable but undeniable. I have come to believe that desperation can come through crisis or cultivation.

God often allows the crisis, but we can also embrace a cultivated desperation.

The prophet Isaiah confessed in desperation, "Woe is me! For I am lost; for I am a man of unclean lips, and I dwell in the midst of a people of unclean lips" (Isa. 6:5). This declaration was not simply motivated by a circumstantial calamity or some low view of himself. It was prompted by a high view of God. Isaiah gave the reason for his passionate confession: "for my eyes have seen the King, the LORD of hosts!" (Isa. 6:5). A consistent pursuit of God's worthiness produces a deepening understanding of our neediness. Cultivated desperation. (We will unpack the full reality of this in chapter 3.)

A CONVICTION ABOUT FOCUSED LEADERSHIP

Returning to the account in Acts 6, we cannot ignore the connection between the Acts 6:7 impact and the Acts 6:4 conviction in the hearts of the apostles. Even though the people were demanding that the leaders fix the widow-feeding problem (Acts 6:1–3), they instead delegated the task to other capable servants so that they could maintain focus on the primary conviction of church leadership. Acts 6:4 clarifies, "But we will devote ourselves to prayer and to the ministry of the word." This direction was affirmed by the church, and seven men were selected to resolve the administrative dilemma.

A CONSISTENT PURSUIT OF GOD'S WORTHINESS PRODUCES A DEEPENING UNDERSTANDING OF OUR NEEDINESS.

This Acts 6:4 tenacity was the essential lifeline for receiving Christ's direction and provision. They recognized that leading the church was a supernatural assignment, not a ministry enterprise. They could not afford to move away from a full and focused experience of Christ's person and presence to instead solve operational problems or implement a new program. Even when the pressing need of the moment held the potential of significant disruption and division, they were resolute.

DEEPER CONVICTION
ABOUT THE HIGHEST PRIORITIES

I've learned after decades of ministry that the prayer level of any congregation never rises higher than the personal example and passion of the church leadership. Conviction must start at the core. Resolute leaders with conviction about prayer always conclude, "Our church must become a 'house of prayer' and we must personally precede it there. We can't point the way, we must lead the way." This conviction fuels life-giving prayer at a personal level, among the staff, the board, the various ministry leaders, and ultimately the entire church.

Today's pastors face pressing dilemmas that can easily derail spiritual focus. The devil does not have to destroy church leaders; he only has to distract them. Times of crisis can accelerate the plethora of distractions. But crisis should ultimately compel leaders to double down on the convictions and ministry priorities that facilitate vital supernatural outcomes.

Leaders know that trying to breathe life into dying programs or driving the creation of new initiatives can consume inordinate amounts of pastoral focus and energy. Managing new demands and unprecedented approaches to ministry in the midst of the chaos of crisis threaten to drain every drop of vitality.

Unlike our highly strategized approach today, the early Acts 6 leaders knew that ministry was received, not achieved. Prayer was not an escape from the pressing predicaments of ministry. Prayer was an engagement with the Head of the church, who alone had the wisdom, direction, power, and unifying grace to resolve thorny problems, undergird necessary focus, and empower weak vessels for powerful gospel impact.

My friend and fellow pastor Keeney Dickenson notes, "We pray in the context of ministry, but Jesus ministered in the context of prayer!"[6] These apostles had seen, felt, and been forever changed by how Christ lived, taught, and implemented the gospel ministry. They were imitating the one who only did what He saw His Father doing, and who lived with divine spiritual insight and power every day, through His life of prayer. They dared not create a different paradigm. They had to walk in His steps through prayer and the ministry of the Word. So must every leader. Jesus did not call us to "figure it all out" but to follow Him.

There has never been a more critical moment in recent history for church leaders to humbly return to the core supernatural realities of ministry. Folks in the pew must also intercede and encourage their leaders to this end. Which leads us to the next core conviction.

A CONVICTION ABOUT
AVAILABILITY TO GOD

Recently, I was speaking to a gathering of faithful believers in Titusville, Florida. While a group of fifty pastors and ministry leaders in their city meet weekly for prayer, these church members assemble in a second location to pray for the pastors. Years earlier, crisis inspired this new commitment to prayer after the discontinuation of the Space Shuttle program, which had been a major economic cornerstone in this city, located adjacent to the Kennedy Space Center.

I challenged these intercessors on their important contribution of supporting their pastors in the work of the gospel, based on the story of Acts 6:1–7. We specifically looked at Acts 6:3: "Therefore, brethren, seek out from among you seven men of good reputation, full of the Holy Spirit and wisdom, whom we may appoint over this business" (NKJV). Many commentators believe this was the beginning of a deacon-type ministry. God used these seven in profound fashion. I reminded these faithful saints that God desired to use them in similar and strategic ways.

For those sensitive to the Spirit during times of crisis,

God issues a call. This is the prompting to a new conviction to be available in service, to step up in meeting practical needs, to pray diligently, and to faithfully support the leadership of the church.

A KEY TO PASTORAL SUCCESS

My friend Leith Anderson, a respected pastor for over three decades, shared with me recently that he believes churches do more to help pastors succeed than pastors do to help churches succeed. This seems very counterintuitive, since we tend to place such great emphasis on the influence of primary leaders. Yet God used this Acts 6 crisis to raise up seven ordinary people for extraordinary influence in the spiritual success of this crucial moment in the early church.

The support of the congregation and the vital help of their seven key representatives in the Acts 6 story proved to be strategic in solving a major problem and restoring unity. Men like Stephen and Phillip appeared on this list. Acts tells us their stories of powerful preaching, evangelism, and even martyrdom. The other five appointees were never again mentioned, but we know God used their lives for His glory in ways that only eternity will reveal.

It is astounding to think that these seven men selected in Acts 6 were somehow identified among thousands of potential candidates based on their stellar Christian reputation. They were notably wise. They were demonstrably controlled by the Holy Spirit. They were devoted to their church. What if we all had the conviction to walk in the same spiritual authenticity and ministry availability of these men?

During your season of crisis, God will likely be calling you to a new commitment to His church—specifically your local church. Don't allow your soul to become overwhelmed by the macro issues of the day, feeling overwhelmed with the frustration of not being able to resolve the complexities of it all. On the other hand, don't become myopic about your own personal struggles (certainly real struggles) such that you miss the reissuing of God's call in the midst of the present chaos.

Our burdens are very real, even overwhelming, in crisis. We must fight for perspective everyday by the renewing of our minds in the Word of God (Rom. 12:1–2). We accept the Lord's invitation to pour our hearts out to Him in earnest prayer, sometimes with tears (Ps. 62:8). Like

Paul, we trust God for sufficient grace to get us through each day (2 Cor. 12:9–10), especially when our prayers for relief seem to be unanswered. We stay in vital fellowship with other believers so that we can bear one another's burdens (Gal. 6:2). But ultimately, we realize that all we are going through is to sanctify us to make us more fruitful in the mission for which the Lord has left us on this broken earth (see Acts 20:22–24).

It has been stated in various ways that if we want to change the world, we need to let the change begin in us. Perhaps this is a moment to ask for a change of heart and to pray like Isaiah, "Here I am! Send me" (Isa. 6:8). Let God speak to you in this crisis to strengthen your walk with Him, your commitment to the local church, and your availablity to answer His unique calling in your life—starting with your vital role in your local congregation. This is a moment to increase your heartfelt, loving prayers for your church leaders. After all, it is hard to be a critic and an intercessor at the same time. Imagine the possibilities of new fruitfulness arising from fresh surrender to God.

THE HOPE OF "SUPERNATURAL MATH"

As we give final consideration to a resetting of essential convictions, I want to suggest a hopeful proposal that I trust will be clear and compelling.

Natural math tells us that $3 + 4 = 7$. As we consider Acts 6, we see a glimpse of what I call supernatural math. Here is the equation:

$$6:3 + 6:4 = 6:7$$

When "Acts 6:3 believers" have a conviction about being fully yielded to God to walk in the Spirit, live wisely, pray earnestly, and support the priorities of "prayer and the ministry of the word" for the church and her leaders, this supernatural equation is formed.

When "Acts 6:4 leaders" are compelled to say *no* to lesser demands so that they can say *yes* to the ultimate convictions of "prayer and the ministry of the word," the possibilities unfold.[7]

Could it be that the combination of $6:3 + 6:4$, rooted in enduring and desperate prayer, would bring us full circle to the hopeful outcome seen in Acts 6:7?[8] Could we believe together that the Word of God will spread powerfully, even during a global moment of crisis? Might we see the number of the disciples multiply greatly while a countless mass of those who had previously been visible and vocal opponents of the faith come to Jesus?

And even if God, in His sovereignty, does not choose to usher in such a moment, we ultimately live with a focus pleasing to Him as we embrace the belief that He could. And in believing that He could, we pray more earnestly, we live more missionally, and we experience a deeper fulfillment that comes from serving a purpose greater than the four walls of our secure existence.

These are the convictions that change our prayers during a crisis. Could we have grace to do more than praying to survive the immediate, but transcend with prayers to thrive in the ultimate mission? Could we cut through the clutter of crisis to conceive that we are called by the Holy Spirit to full participation in a supernatural advancement of the gospel?

In the context of these current calamities—perhaps especially now—let's determine to let God embed vital convictions in our souls. God is able, if we are willing.

NOTE: In Appendix 1, I have outlined a dream for 100,000 Agents of Renewal. It is a vision of 100,000 leaders and church members who are consistently, tangibly, and enduringly committed to some core grace-empowered responsibilities that undergird our calling to supernatural outcomes. I hope you will join me in clarifying and committing to these essential practices.

DEVOTE YOURSELF TO A CONSISTENT EXPERIENCE OF PRAYING IN **COMMUNITY**[1]

The condition of the church may be very accurately gauged by its prayer meetings. So is the prayer meeting a grace-ometer, and from it we may judge of the amount of divine working among a people. If God be near a church, it must pray. And if He be not there, one of the first tokens of His absence will be slothfulness in prayer.
Charles Spurgeon

There has never been a spiritual awakening in any country or locality that did not begin in united prayer.
A. T. Pierson

During the COVID-19 pandemic, many Christians were prohibited from meeting together in their normal worship gatherings, small groups, and other ministry activities. As the weeks dragged on, the fellowship void became deeply discouraging for many. While online services and meetings provided significant opportunities for connection, it was just not the same as real in-person interaction.

During that period, I was privileged to coach over a dozen groups of pastors from across the world. These church leaders all sensed that God was using this time to create a fresh biblical hunger for community with other believers—and especially a reset of praying together with fresh passion, transparency, interdependence, and consistency.

WALKING IN COMMUNITY

I believe one of God's great intentions in our trials is to draw us deeper into life-giving community with other believers. And, one of the richest and most rewarding aspects of community comes when we pray together in meaningful heart-to-heart connection. Yet, this is a clear uphill climb for our independent, individualistic, and guarded tendencies.

If you were to ask, "Which is more important—private prayer or corporate prayer?" my answer will always be "yes!" It is like asking which leg is more crucial to walking, the right or the left?

In the early church, they understood the value of community, meeting together *daily* in prayer and the other vital disciplines for spiritual growth. In Acts 2:42 we see the discipleship patterns that emerged immediately in the Jerusalem church, comprised almost entirely of new believers. It says, "And they continued steadfastly in the apostles' doctrine and fellowship, in the breaking of bread, and in prayers" (NKJV).

You could not learn the apostles' doctrine by listening to podcasts by Peter, James, or John. You had to be gathered in community. The same was obviously true of fellowship and the breaking of bread. And how did they learn to pray? Together.

These prayers were not just a blessing tacked on to the beginning and end of Bible study. These early Christians gathered exclusively for prayer. In all likelihood they followed the pattern Jesus set forth (as we will see in the next chapter).

The church was birthed in a ten-day prayer meeting (see Acts 1:14, 2:1). They coped with crisis and persecution, together on their knees (Acts 4:24–31). As the church grew, the apostles refused to become embroiled in administrative problems because of their resolute desire to model prayer in their leadership team (Acts 6:4). Through united prayer, they trusted God for miraculous divine interventions in times of extreme trouble (Acts 12:5–12). They received ministry direction through intense seasons of worshipful prayer (Acts 13:1–2).

THOSE WHO NEGLECT THE CONSISTENT HABIT OF PRAYING IN EXTENDED FASHION WITH A COMMUNITY OF BELIEVERS ARE ROBBING THEMSELVES OF GREAT BLESSING AND BALANCE.

What a contrast to our individualistic culture. We have been taught that prayer is something to do almost exclusively on our own in a "prayer closet" somewhere. In reality, early Christians learned to pray largely by praying together.

Personally, I cannot imagine living a vibrant and balanced Christian life without a regular dose of both. Those who neglect the consistent habit of praying in extended fashion with a community of believers are robbing themselves of great blessing and balance. In a sense, they are trying to hop on one leg and finding the prayer journey difficult, at best.

ISOLATED BY INDIVIDUALISM

"Why have we neglected the corporate emphasis on prayer found in . . . Acts and the Epistles?" Gene Getz, noted professor from Dallas Seminary, asks that question in his book *Praying for One Another* and notes how we view biblical prayer from our bias rather than from the original intent and context of the Scriptures. He notes that our Western culture is distinguished by rugged individualism, and makes this observation:

We use the personal pronouns "I" and "my" and "me." We have not been taught to think in terms of "we" and "our" and "us." Consequently, we individualize many references to corporate experience in the New Testament, thus often emphasizing personal prayer. More is said in Acts and the Epistles about corporate prayer, corporate learning of biblical truth, corporate evangelism, and corporate Christian maturity and growth than about the personal aspects of these Christian disciplines.

Don't misunderstand. Both are intricately related. But the personal dimensions of Christianity are difficult to maintain and practice consistently unless they grow out of a proper corporate experience on a regular basis.[2]

In our Western culture, we have come to believe that it is more important to pray alone than with others. This is a symptom of our basic view of society. In his book *The Connecting Church*, Randy Frazee describes our culture of "individualism." He notes that we are no longer born into a culture of community but a "way of life that makes the individual supreme or sovereign over everything."[3] Frazee documents this as a problem, especially for those born after World War II. He laments the impact on the church by observing that we have "all too often mirrored the culture by making Christianity an individual sport."[4]

GROUP INSTRUCTION

We know the Lord's Prayer is a model for the *content* of our praying. We should also embrace it as a model for the *context* of our prayers. Jesus said to His followers in Matthew 6:5, "And when you pray . . ." He assumed they would gather in prayer as a regular part of their spiritual development. The pronoun here is plural, as He is talking to them as a group about their engagement together in prayer. In our language, it would be like saying "when you guys pray" or "when y'all pray." In other words, Jesus says, "When you all pray together as my followers, do it this way in your gatherings, not like those praise-hungry Pharisees or misguided Gentiles."

To support this idea, the pronouns are all plural in the pattern of prayer He gave. He did not give the instruction to pray, "*My* Father who art in heaven . . . give *me* this day *my* daily bread, and forgive *me my* sins, lead *me* not into temptation, but deliver *me* from evil . . ." This was a teaching passage on the mindset, motives, venue, and pattern of corporate praying in the lives of Jesus' followers. As Albert Mohler has aptly noted,

There is no first-person singular pronoun in the entire prayer! . . .

One of the besetting sins of evangelicalism is our obsession with individualism. This obsession with individualism chronically besets us as evangelicals. The first-person singular pronoun reins in our thinking. We tend to think about nearly everything (including the truths of God's Word) only as they relate to *me*. This is why when Jesus teaches his disciples to pray, he emphasizes from the very outset that we are part of a corporate people called the church.[5]

IDENTIFYING OUR INDIVIDUALISTIC INCLINATIONS

Today we read the commands about prayer in the New Testament Epistles and assume they are primarily designed to motivate the individual believer in his or her private prayer time. We have come to believe that prayer is first and best experienced at a private level; for some of the zealots, it might be an activity they will enjoy in concert with others. Yet early Christians had a very different perspective.

We must keep in mind that until the advent of the printing press, almost all learning was verbal and in community settings. This clearly affected the way believers received and applied the truth. Today, with individual copies of the Bible, we make the applications first privately, then corporately, if at all. This is a great spiritual loss.

Even many of our songs are dominated by the personal pronouns *I*, *me*, and *my*. Since we are singing in community it would seem most appropriate to incorporate *we*, *our*, and *us*. This is just another example of how individualism trumps community in such a subtle manner.

In New Testament times, a letter would arrive from Paul and believers had but one choice in order to receive this truth. They had to gather in community, as there were no individual printed copies of the Scripture. And when a command was read to the assembled believers in the original language, the plural pronouns popped. The application to believers as a community was clear. As a result, they prayed together often, passionately, and obediently.

Michael Griffiths reiterates this consideration when he writes,

In standard English, the second person singular "you" and the second person plural "you" are identical. Thus, New Testament Letters addressed to congregations are read (by us) as though they were addressed to the individuals. It is good and right that we should apply the Scriptures to ourselves personally, but it is unfortunate if we also apply the Scriptures individualistically and ignore the fact that the original intention was to instruct us not so much as individuals, but as whole communities of Christian people.[6]

One very unfortunate Western application of the text involves the idea of the "closet." When Jesus said "enter into thy closet" to pray (Matt. 6:6 KJV), just what did He mean? We usually assume it is a small cubicle designed for shoes, clothes, a flashlight, and a kneeling prayer warrior.

This word *tamion* appears in the Greek New Testament four times. Among those instances, it can mean "inner rooms" (Luke 12:3 NASB) or a "storeroom" (Luke 12:24 NASB, NIV). Most major translations, other than the KJV, use a clearer idea when they describe this place of group prayer in Matthew 6:6, calling it a *room* or *inner room*. One thing is clear: the narrow interpretation of a private chamber for solitary prayer is not a necessary or reasonable meaning. This would be especially difficult when Jesus speaks to a group of disciples, using plural pronouns. It would either be a very crowded private closet with many sweaty and cramping disciples—or it must mean a place large enough for a corporate gathering.

The obvious historical application of this principle is seen in Acts 1:12–2:1, where the disciples are gathered in secret in an upper room, out of the public eye, enjoying extended group prayer. This pattern of praying together continued in Acts as they responded to persecution (Acts 4:23–31), engaged in intercession for an imprisoned leader (12:12–17), and sought the Lord's direction for ministry (13:1–3).

HOW WE LEARN

Many believers struggle in learning how to pray. Hundreds of volumes have been written over the centuries on the theology and practice of prayer. Yet the most fundamental principle has often been neglected. Young Christians must learn to pray in community with mature believers. We all (even pastors) learn to pray by praying with others who know how to pray. D. A. Carson has affirmed this dynamic: "Many facets of Christian discipleship, not least prayer, are rather more effectively passed on by modeling than by formal teaching. Good praying is more easily caught than taught. . . . We should choose models from whom we can learn."[7]

Prayer is vital for transformation, and corporate prayer is indispensable for a truly New Testament church with supernatural impact.

IF I WERE THE DEVIL

In a devotional titled "If I Were the Devil,"[8] I wrote that while the devil is not all-knowing, he is shrewd from countless years of experience. He certainly knows some things. He knows the Bible (see James 2:19, Matt. 4:6), so he knows the divine game plan for his defeat—and the vital role of prayer.

He knows church history. He is fully aware that his greatest defeats have come during seasons of spiritual awakening and revival and that every one of these seasons of exponential spiritual transformation has been rooted in movements of united, biblical prayer.

He also knows human nature. He observes our tendency to live independently of God's supernatural provision for our lives. He was active in Laodicea, for example, as he assisted that church in living by their own riches, efforts, and sufficiency rather than pursuing intimacy with their Savior (see Rev. 3:15–17). He likes things this way.

Yes, I believe our spiritual enemy is using his deceptive strategies to keep Christians from praying in transforming ways—and especially keep them from praying together. He keeps us busy and isolated from one another. He does everything possible to keep us distracted and disinterested in biblical, balanced, worship-based prayer gatherings—thwarting spiritual awaking at all costs. As long as Christians are sincere but isolated, active but powerless, entertained but shallow—he wins. And he loves it so.

JESUS' PLAN:
UNITED IN TRANSFORMATION

In spite of the devil's malevolent intentions, the Lord Jesus has a triumphant, supernatural plan, and we must embrace it with resolve. In Mark 11:17, Jesus made His intentions clear, "Then He taught, saying to them, 'Is it not written, 'My house shall be called a house of prayer for all nations'? But you have made it a 'den of thieves'" (NKJV). Jesus knew the kind of power He was able to unleash in humble, dependent people who would allow Him to bear the fruit of His life and power through prayer. Again, that is why He started the church with His people on their knees. He sustained and blessed the church the same way. Still today, He wants His church to be characterized by an environment of life-giving prayer.

Paul, when instructing the young pastor Timothy in how to establish church function and order, made the priority of prayer very clear again. He wrote, "Therefore I exhort *first of all* that supplications, prayers, intercessions, and giving of thanks be made for all men" (1 Tim. 2:1 NKJV, emphasis added). This was a clear reference to the priority of the gathered people of God. Prayer was not supposed to be the only thing the church did, just the first thing they did. That's the way Jesus wanted it to be.

THE "WHY" BEHIND THE "WHERE"

Ultimately, prayer is for the glory of God. Paul expounded on the goal of the church gathered, crying out to God in prayer. He wrote,

While you also cooperate by your prayers for us [helping and laboring together with us]. Thus [the lips of] many persons [turned toward God will eventually] give thanks on our behalf for the grace (the blessing of deliverance) granted us at the request of the many who have prayed. (2 Cor. 1:11 AMPC)

Paul explains that when we pray together, and bear collective witness to His answers to prayer, God receives greater thanksgiving. He is glorified and our thanksgiving is greater because we have prayed together.

When we gather to pray in a worship-based fashion, not only is God glorified in our very act of collective adoration, but He will also be glorified in our ongoing recognition of His transforming power, both in and through us, as He advances His gospel and glory in this world. Even a global pandemic can't stop that.

EVALUATING RITUAL AND ROUTINE TO EMBRACE REALITY

The disruption of the COVID-19 pandemic prompted church leaders across all spectrums to ask hard questions about the elements of Christian worship that needed to be reevaluated and the aspects that needed to be reprioritized. Rituals and routines that had become commonplace were suddenly gone and seen with a fresh sense of examination. Suddenly, things that seemed so essential were exposed as quite incidental. In the conversations I had with scores of pastors, a fresh realization of the need for united prayer as a core component of Christian community was front and center. It would be just like God to strip away the superficial forms in order to draw us back to the functions that are truly scriptural and supernatural.

Clearly we have more tools for ministry today than at any time in church history. There is nothing inherently wrong with all of our educational, leadership, facility, and technological tools. But there is a difference between simply *using* the tools and *depending* on the tools. The acid test of our authentic dependence is the passionate, tangible prayer commitment of the leadership and the people. One of the redeeming effects of a nationwide crisis is the opportunity God gives us to discern any and all of our misguided dependencies in order to return with Spirit-guided courage to the realities that have always promoted transformation and propelled the gospel in world-shaking fashion.

THE KEY TO CHANGE

In the 1860s, Pastor Charles Spurgeon led prayer meetings at the Metropolitan Tabernacle. People met at 7:00 a.m. and 7:30 p.m. every day. More than three thousand came to the meeting on Monday evening. One evening a visitor asked why Spurgeon's ministries were so successful. Spurgeon walked his visitor to the sanctuary, opened the door, and let him watch the participants. Nothing more needed to be said.[9] Spurgeon's conviction was clear, "We shall never see much change for the better in our churches in general till the prayer meeting occupies a higher place in the esteem of Christians."[10]

Lewis O. Thompson, a college professor and pastor from the 1800s wrote, "If it is true that the active piety of a church rises no higher than it manifests itself in the prayer-meeting, so that here, as on a barometer, all changes in spiritual life are faithfully recorded, then certainly too much attention cannot be given by both pastor and people to the conduct of the prayer-meeting."[11]

OVERCOMING OPPOSITION—TOGETHER

Jonathan Edwards, having witnessed the effects of the Great Awakening, wrote a now-famous treatise in defense of this spiritual movement.[12] He believed in the undeniable need for united prayer in view of an extraordinary work of the Spirit. Edwards understood and urged the reality that concerted, united, passionate prayer was always linked to revival. This is God's plan. This is one of the devil's primary strategies—to keep Christians from praying together.

What could be more crucial for such a time as this? And what opportunity could be better than now to evaluate how we pray in order to align our approach with a biblical, life-giving pattern so that we might pray together better and more biblically?

DEVELOP YOUR BIBLICAL, LIFE-GIVING PRAYER **COMPETENCY**[1]

We restore prayer to its context in God's word. Prayer is not something we think up to get God's attention or enlist his favor. Prayer is answering speech. The first word is God's word. Prayer is a human word and is never the first word, never the primary word, never the initiating and shaping word simply because we are never first; never primary. . . . The first word everywhere and always is God's word to us, not ours to him.
Eugene Peterson

Just as God's Word must reform our theology, our ethics, and our practices so also must it reform our praying.
D. A. Carson

God desires to use crisis to awaken His people to a new captivation and competency in prayer. He will shake us up to wake us up from our spiritual slumber to a fresh spiritual pursuit. Perhaps our greatest yearning in a difficult season should not be, "Lord, deliver me from this trial" or "Show me how to fix it all" but rather "Teach me to pray."

Yet truth be told, many of us struggle to pray effectively and enduringly. Our time with God is invaded by technological distractions. Our minds drift in and out. We mumble through our drowsiness and feel guilty about our lack of discipline and devotion.

The church prayer meeting is often the least attended gathering of the week. Personally, I grew up with an aversion to prayer. My parents dragged me to the old-fashioned midweek prayer meeting at church. While these faithful intercessors were sincere, their approach to prayer—comprised largely of long lists of mostly physical needs—did not capture my heart, nor the hearts of the majority of the church. I could not help but ask, "Is there a better way? A more biblical way?"

After decades of pastoral ministry, leading multiple prayer meetings every week, I have concluded that

God is not the author of boredom, especially when we are conversing with Him. I have been in prayer meetings (and even led some) where participants snored, snorted, drooled, and fell over, while taking a prayer nap. In my book *PRAYzing!: Creative Prayer Experiences from A to Z,* I declare war on sleepy prayer times. If prayer lacks creativity, energy, and innovation, it is not God's fault; it is ours.[2]

Admittedly, we've all engaged in some supplication siestas. Even Peter, James, and John dozed on Jesus, first on the Mount of Transfiguration and later on the Mount of Olives (Luke 9:32; Matt. 26:36–42). Like Jesus' inner circle, our spirit is willing, but our flesh is weak. Yet the New Testament commands us to be watchful, wakeful, and alert in prayer (Eph. 6:18; Col. 4:2; 1 Peter 4:7).

How do we find the keys to energized, engaging prayer? As a pastor, my frustration with lethargic, dozy gatherings has motivated me to try and learn more about how to avoid these dead-in-the-water prayer times. Over the years, I have embraced valuable lessons about creative approaches to prayer. There is still much to learn, but this chapter will help us all to avoid zoning out in our intercession and embrace a model that could spring forth in renewed transformation as we learn to seek God's face.

HOW *NOT* TO START A PRAYER TIME

The opening moments of any prayer gathering often set the trajectory for the entire experience. How we start the prayer time is a core factor in its effectiveness.

Over the years, I've heard it and done it: "Does anyone have any prayer requests?" Don't start here. This establishes an immediate human-centered, rather than God-centered, experience. Further, it is hard to be an "equal opportunity provider." After Uncle Charlie, Aunt Matilda, and Billy Bob share a long list of ailing body parts, friends traveling on vacation, and third cousins in crises five states away, no one else has the time (or desire) to unload all their needs. Time is limited and precious. Of course, this starting point is not a good stewardship of time in any case, because after participants have described in detail all the assortment of needs, we circle back and pray about it all again. (If there is any time left actually to pray.)

Another traditional approach is to begin by saying, "Let's just pray as we feel led." The intention, I suppose, is an urging to be led by the Spirit in our prayers. Somehow this gets lost in translation and is interpreted, "Just pray whatever comes to your mind." What ensues is typically a disconnected flurry of impulses based on the experience of the day or pressing frustration of the moment. Not a good place to start.

Commonly, we might even announce, "Let's just pray around the circle." This is unhelpful as participants are forced to pray because it is "their turn," whether the Spirit is really prompting them or not. Introverts freeze up, especially when the person just before them in the circle extrapolates a prolonged King-James-Only prayer speech. Of course, if you are the last person in the circle, you either agree with all that has been said since everyone has already stolen your prayer material, or you endeavor to come up with some additional content so as not to appear unspiritual.

THE EIGHT GUIDING PRINCIPLES FOR EXPERIENCING LIFE-GIVING PRAYER EXPERIENCES

How do we avoid a false start? What are the keys to launching and sustaining a dynamic prayer experience? Here are eight guidelines that consistently help me as I facilitate prayer. The first four are applicable to either personal or corporate prayer:

1. *Foundation*

I start virtually all of my personal and corporate prayer times with an open Bible. This serves as the foundation for prayer. I call this Scripture-fed prayer.

Prayer is two-way conversation. So, then, who should start the conversation? This is important because in most dialogue, the person that starts the conversation tends to guide it. Our choice depends on our understanding of true prayer. If prayer is our opportunity to barge into God's presence to inform Him of all that He needs to do to structure the universe according to our specifications for a happy and comfortable life, then we should start the conversation. Instead, if prayer is about knowing His will, trusting His grace, and joining Him in His purposes, then we should let Him start the conversation. This requires open Bibles.

Speaking about this very idea, pastor John Piper notes, "What I have seen is that those whose prayers are most saturated with Scripture are generally most fervent and most effective in prayer. And where the mind isn't brimming with the Bible, the heart is not generally brimming with prayer."[3] George Müller (the renowned man of faith and evangelist who cared for thousands of orphans and established dozens of Christian schools in the 1800s) spoke about the vital role of Scripture in his prayer life. He noted that for years he tried to pray without starting in the Bible in the morning. Inevitably, his mind wandered, sometimes for ten, fifteen, even thirty minutes.[4] Then, when he began to start each morning with the Bible to nourish his soul, he found his heart being transformed by the truth, resulting in spontaneous prayers of confession, thanksgiving, intercession, and supplication. This became his daily experience for decades, resulting in great personal growth and power for life and ministry.

2. *Fervor*

This is the element of Spirit-led prayer apart from which prayer is impossible. While we know this, we cannot forget the vital, practical role of the Spirit in our united prayers. He is the one who inspired the Scriptures and He lives in us to explain what He meant by what He said so that we can understand, apply, and fully experience its power, especially as we pray. Accordingly, it is imperative to engage in an intentional focus and reliance upon the Holy Spirit at the outset of every prayer experience. We know He is our indwelling prayer tutor who leads us in prayer that is God-aligned and reassuring—and that ultimately conforms us to Christ and leads to God's glory (Rom. 8:26–30).

3. *Faith*

A worship-based faith transforms the nature of all united prayer. Hebrews 11:6 reminds us, "And without faith it is impossible to please him, for whoever would draw near to God must believe that he exists and that he rewards those who seek him." This vital requirement of faith in prayer is focused on the reality and character of God, knowing He rewards those who *seek* Him. Don't miss that focus. *Seeking Him,* not just presenting long lists of needs—appealing to His hand, but a passion to pursue His face first and foremost.

4. *Focus*

With this establishment of Scripture-fed, Spirit-led, worship-based prayer, now we must lead with a biblical and balanced focus. Jesus gave the clear pattern. This is not just something to be quoted by memory but to be experienced corporately. (Again, notice all the plural pronouns.)

Pray then like this:

> "Our Father in heaven,
> hallowed be your name.
> Your kingdom come,
> your will be done,
>   on earth as it is in heaven.
> Give us this day our daily bread,
> and forgive us our debts,
>   as we also have forgiven our debtors.
> And lead us not into temptation,
>   but deliver us from evil." (Matt. 6:9–13)

When Jesus said, "Pray then like this," it was not just a suggestion or one of many options. In the Greek language, it is a "present imperative." This was His command toward a consistent experience of this biblical pattern, for our good and His glory as we pray.

In following this pattern, I see first a very simple approach but then also a more comprehensive experience. Most fundamentally, there are two parts to the prayer. The first half is entirely Godward. The second half is human-centric. I like to capture this two-part rhythm with this descriptor: "He is worthy. We are needy." Even if there is only a short amount of time to pray, when we start with a passage of Scripture and then engage in a pure articulation of worship, participants are captured by His worthiness, and moving to a time of trusting Him with our needs is natural. Our requests are informed and inspired by our worship.

A more comprehensive breakdown of the prayer is focused on four movements. I describe them as Reverence, Response, Requests, and Readiness. Using the 4/4 pattern (adapted from my musical background) and following the exact themes of the model prayer, it looks like this:

THE 4/4 PATTERN FOR PRAYER

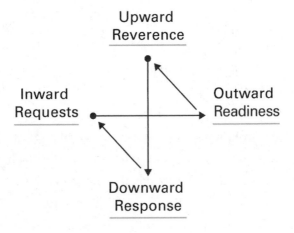

Upward
Reverence

Inward
Requests

Outward
Readiness

Downward
Response

With an open Bible, the beginning point in prayer is to ask, "Who is God?" and "What does He reveal about Himself in this passage?" This sparks worship (reverence) in alignment with the focus, "Our Father in heaven, hallowed be your name."

Since worship is the response of all I am to the revelation of all He is, the next movement is an expression of surrender, submission, or confession—in alignment with His will. "Your kingdom come, your will be done, on earth as it is in heaven" guides us to yield our motives, our mind, our agenda, and our behavior to His purposes. This is prompted by the question, "How do You want me to respond?" and is often guided by a verse in the passage.

"Give us this day our daily bread, and forgive us our debts, as we also have forgiven our debtors" answers the question, "What should we pray about?" Participants can allow the Scripture to guide their requests in connection to both resource needs and relationship needs, as Jesus' model prayer indicates.

In the final movement we find a focus on readiness for spiritual battle. Where do we go from here? What will we face today in a sinful and hostile world? As the pattern indicates, "And lead us not into temptation, but deliver us from evil." Praying from the Scripture is especially vital at this point, as the best way to overcome the attacks of the enemy is with the memorized and spoken Word of God (see Matt. 4:1–10, Eph. 6:17).

Our ministry, Strategic Renewal, provides many resources to help you understand and lead biblical, balanced, life-giving prayer times. We do this through online coaching cohorts[5] as well as other training resources.[6] The following principles are specifically helpful in facilitating and participating in prayer in a group.

5. *Flow*

The real challenge in leading a prayer time is to facilitate the participation of the people so that all things are done for edification. Sometimes this can feel like herding squirrels. To guide a flow of prayer that reflects continuity, agreement, unity, and blessing, I follow what I call the "ABCs" of prayer:

Audible—This seems so elementary, but participants must be reminded to pray loudly enough that others can hear. In group prayer, there is no point in opening one's mouth if the others cannot hear. We need to hear what the Spirit is prompting in others. Hearing another believer as they pray enables me to know their heart in a deeper way and prompts things in me that I need to pray about. It fosters a collective sense of understanding and agreement. It can even teach me to pray more effectively, especially when the other person is further down the road in their walk with Christ.

Brief—I've been in many a prayer time when I wanted to tap someone on the shoulder and ask, "Does your train of thought have a caboose or not?" Long, protracted, scattered prayers have a way of sucking the life out of a prayer time. Violators may need to be encouraged in private toward a more measured participation. Many of the long-winded folks in prayer meetings are spiritually sincere, just not socially aware.

Clear—Guiding participants to pray clearly about one thing at a time encourages greater agreement and focus. When someone dumps a load of seventeen different requests, it creates confusion as the others do not know which one of the many disconnected appeals to agree with. An effectively led prayer time allows people to pray multiple times but preferably about one thing at a time.

Providing distinct entry points helps facilitate this. Our ministry website has many examples of this idea of praying from the Scriptures with balanced focus and edifying continuity.[7]

6. *Freedom*

Too many times, we lead prayer experiences where participants sit comfortably in a padded chair or pew, with head bowed and eyes closed. This posture can be a surefire recipe for drifting minds and sleeping bodies. It is helpful to give permission (even encouragement) to participants to stand, walk, kneel, or even lay prostrate. Eyes can be opened, and should be when praying from the Scriptures. I say to people, "You can lift your hands, sit on your hands, clap your hands, look at your hands, and even smell your hands—whatever. Just stay physically engaged to allow the body to transmit the expression of the soul."

7. *Flexibility*

Over the years, with the Lord's help, I have created thousands of Scripture-fed prayer guides that were compiled in preparation for corporate prayer gatherings. However, we know that while the Spirit can direct ahead of time He also prompts an unanticipated focus in the moment. The point is simply to prayerfully and thoughtfully plan, as necessary, but to hold the plan loosely, knowing there is a unique dynamic that occurs when believers get together and pray.

8. *Faithfulness*

Leading in prayer is a lifelong calling, not a short-term fix. We must embrace a mindset of leading for the long haul. I remember a number of years ago after more than a decade of intense prayer leadership, crying out to the Lord, "How long do I have to keep up this 'prayer thing'?" In a clear way, the Lord directed my heart to a penetrating question, challenging me to endurance: "Daniel, how long will you brush your teeth, take a shower, eat breakfast, and get dressed?" I understood. It was as if the Lord said, "Why would you question the longevity of this paramount commitment any more than these other basic lifelong routines?" That settled it for me.

Since then, I resolved that the consistent pursuit of spiritual intimacy and influence in prayer ministry is my way of life until my final day on earth. I tell believers everywhere I go that they need to develop a dream of dying on their knees. My dream, and I hope yours as well, is to seek spiritual intimacy at a personal level and lead fellow believers humbly into His presence until my last day. Finish the course!

KEYS TO FACILITATING EFFECTIVE AND EDIFYING GROUP PARTICIPATION

Beyond these guidelines, here are some practical insights that will help in the effectiveness of a corporate prayer experience:

Allow for a Variety of Participation

While praying "out loud" brings positive benefit, I never require people to pray aloud. Being a strong extrovert, I do not understand it, but some people get exceedingly stressed over the idea of articulating what is in their hearts in the company of other people.

I like to get people praying together, sometimes in pairs, triplets, or other groupings. However, I always allow the freedom for someone to simply pray alone or exclusively with a spouse or friend with whom they feel more comfortable.

Level the Praying Ground

When praying from the Scriptures, I love to give people a track to run on. The goal is to guide the group in praying with as much clarity and application as possible. Accordingly, I find it helpful to give specific entry points that allow people to finish the sentence or fill in the blank. Helping participants consider specific reasons, times, or circumstances is often a very encouraging tool. Examples include prayer expressions like:

"Lord, thank You that You were faithful when . . ."

- You woke me up this morning to a new day to trust You.
- You empower me to overcome my addiction to drugs.
- You forgave and cleansed me after a season of rebellion during my college years.
- You empowered me to finish my schooling in spite of my weariness.

"Lord, You are great because . . ."

- You are the Creator of the universe.
- You have done awesome deeds throughout history.
- You number and name the stars of heaven.
- You are the King of kings and Lord of lords.

"Thank You that You love me, even though . . ."
- I have sinned against You so often.
- I often do not comprehend Your great love.
- I don't always act in sacrificial love toward my family and friends.

"I'm feeling fearful about _____; give me grace to trust You."

"I pray for my friend _____, that I would see him or her come to saving faith."

"Give me faith to trust You with my children this week, especially when . . ."

"My friend _____ needs Your special grace because . . ."

The options are endless, especially when the prompts come right from the truths of Scripture. While this may seem very simplistic, the net effect is that it "levels the praying ground." Long-winded people who struggle to find their punctuation are guided to pray specific, focused prayers. Introverts are enabled to participate without feeling like they have to come up with some highly conceptual prayer speech. Long-term believers are encouraged to be more transparent and practical in their prayers. New believers find it easy to join in with these simple points of guidance.

SUFFICIENT WORD AND SPIRIT

Beyond these practical recommendations, the bottom line is that the Word and Spirit are fully sufficient to equip us to pray and to lead others in prayer. Pastor Cliff Boone leads Cedar Crest Bible Fellowship Church in Allentown, Pennsylvania, where he has served as senior pastor since 2002. He recently completed one of our pastoral coaching cohorts as part of his growing awakening to the priority of prayer in church ministry. As a champion of expository preaching, Cliff has been awakened to the equal priority of prayer. In a recent interview, Cliff pondered, "How could I have missed the priority the Scripture gives to corporate prayer? Now, I never feel more like a pastor than after I have led my people in a prayer meeting. That had been a missing piece of ministry for many years. Before, as I led my people in prayer I always felt inadequate, but now I say, 'This is going to be great. It's a whole new ballgame.'" Boone testifies that the blanks have been filled in and speaks of his constant two-part prayer, "Lord teach me to pray, and teach me to teach my people how to pray."[8] This is pastoring as it ought to be in essential conviction of "prayer and the ministry of the word."

This is a necessary commitment and competency available to every believer who seriously desires to see God redeem a present crisis to ignite a viral commitment to prayer that will transform hearts, homes, and communities by the power of the Holy Spirit.

DETERMINE YOU'LL BECOME SPIRITUALLY **CONTAGIOUS**[1]

The key to a new movement of the Spirit of God will not be in a new technique, but in the "old" paths of Gospel proclamation, earnest prayer, and yearning for the Spirit.[2]
J. D. Greear

We cannot stop telling about everything we have seen and heard.
Acts 4:20 (NLT)

During the COVID-19 pandemic, the entire world was upended by an unseen, rapidly spreading contagion. It became deadly to hundreds of thousands of lives and, by extension, destructive to countless livelihoods. I need say no more. We all know and have tried to navigate through this wearisome chapter in history.

But the idea of contagion can also have a positive meaning. Merriam-Webster offers these alternative definitions: "contagious influence, quality, or nature," "rapid communication of an influence (such as a doctrine or emotional state)," "an influence that spreads rapidly."[3]

I think of many things that are contagious, both positive and negative. The unrestrained laughter of a child. The enthusiastic cheering of a crowd at a sports event when their team wins a close game. A yawn. Emotions of joy or fear. A juicy, hot-off-the-press nugget of gossip. The uncontrolled anger of a rioting crowd.

I want to flip our common idea of contagion on its head and inspire you with the positive hope of a truly holy and contagious work of God. If, during any crisis, we embrace fresh conviction, engage in biblical, praying community, and equip ourselves in a new prayer competency, we could very well see a global contagion of Spirit-birthed renewal and inexplicable gospel impact. Some have called it "revival." Others speak of an "awakening." Whatever terms we use, I pray we can dream of the possibilities. A world in crisis needs Christians on a mission.

BEYOND "REVIVAL"

Not long ago, I chauffeured a well-known pastor to the airport after he finished preaching at a leadership conference. He has written extensively and is highly respected by pastors around the world from a wide variety of theological persuasions.

As we drove, we wandered onto the topic of revival, speaking affectionately of various individuals and ministries. Midstream, he nonchalantly inserted a riveting statement, "You know, revival is not even taught in the New Testament." I was stunned. I knew this was in no way a dismissal of our need for prayer or any lack of emphasis on the Holy Spirit. Rather, it was an honest observation from a truth-loving student of the Bible who is not beholden to any particular denomination, philosophy, or stream of church methodology.

For weeks, I could not shake his statement. It dawned on me that easily 90 percent of the messages I have heard or the books I have read on "revival" are rooted in teachings and stories from the Old Testament. They were based on God's dealings with His people under the old covenant, before the cross, before all the benefits of the finished work of Christ, before the outpouring of the

Holy Spirit at Pentecost, and before the new reality of the indwelling of the Holy Spirit in the lives of His children. I began to think about my own sermons on revival. Certainly they were sincere and passionate—but based on the Old Testament.

After a careful search, it was confirmed. I could not find the word "revival" in the New Testament. At best, the concept could be extrapolated here and there.[4] I was called to an honest evaluation of much of what I have said and taught about revival.

To be "revived" is "to return to consciousness or life" and "become active or flourishing again."[5] Concerning the actual word "revival," Bill Hull has noted,

> The word is thrown around as if we all know what it means. There is a consensus across the theological spectrum that revival means to fully experience the fulfillment of both the Great Commandment and that the Great Commission, but expectations and descriptions of the revival manifestations vary greatly. . . . Revival is simply a term we have given to the special activity of God throughout history. . . . Spiritual revival (the idea) is in the Bible. Being

radically transformed by the power of God based on the finished work of the resurrected Christ is in the Bible. Whatever it is called, revived, renewed, refreshed, regenerated, liberated, empowered, filled, raised, or healed, I'm for it![6]

Yet, he notes,

It is dangerous to give the variety of spiritual experiences in Scripture one label, namely "revival" and then canonize it as the only hope for the church, the nation, and all of humankind. This leads to reliance on God to do all the work—not only his but ours. All spiritual work is God's work, I know that, but Jesus left over 200 commands for his church. Our desperation for revival as a solution is in part evidence of our failure to walk daily in the power of the Spirit and to obey what God has already paid for and equipped us to do.[7]

From a New Testament standpoint, could it be that what we label, long for, and labor over (i.e., "revival") is really an extraordinary sensitivity, surrender, and obedience to the Holy Spirit? Perhaps we could just say that what we really desire is that every believer, every church, every ministry become undeniably, supernaturally contagious by the power of the Holy Spirit for the sake of the gospel.

As Norman Grubb has stated, in his extraordinary book, *Continuous Revival*, "Indeed, revival is really just obeying the Holy Spirit."[8] Instead of praying for "revival" (whatever that might mean in our mind at the time) we might be clearer to pray for "an extraordinary understanding of an obedience to the indwelling power of the Holy Spirit." Either way, I think we all want the same thing. Clearly, the Spirit's promises and presence must become the focus of our desire for an extraordinary work of God. Steven Olford concurs, "One of the determining factors in seeing a church-wide revival is the determination to fulfill all of God's purposes righteously *in the power of the Holy Spirit.*"[9]

> GOD DOES NOT NEED A PROSPEROUS CHURCH. RATHER, HE DESIRES A PURE, PRAYING, AND POWERFUL CHURCH—FILLED WITH THE HOLY SPIRIT.

I love Norman Grubb's description: "The truth is that revival is really *the Reviver in action,* and He came two thousand years ago at Pentecost. Revival is not so much a vertical outpouring from heaven (for the Reviver is *already* here in His temple, the bodies of the redeemed) as it is a horizontal outmoving of the Reviver through these temples into the world. It is a *horizontal* rather than a *vertical* movement."[10]

WHY?

I believe we must examine *why* we desire this kind of holy, spiritual contagion. I fear that many of us pray for revival secretly hoping that this spiritual work might turn back the clock and the culture to the day when we all sat on the front porch, eating homemade apple pie, reading our Bibles, going to Sunday school, and voting for conservative values.

However, I am becoming increasingly convinced that if we experience revival, we might not go forward into a new Christian golden age, but rather, into martyrdom. When the Holy Spirit is working powerfully through a gospel-embracing people, a hostile society reacts in force. But not to worry. God does not need a prosperous church. Rather, He desires a pure, praying, and powerful church—filled with the Holy Spirit. Bold. Sacrificial. Fully committed. Contagious. Declaring with abandon that to live is Christ and to die is gain. That was the DNA of the early church. They did not cling to any promise of religious freedom but understood the inevitability of persecution. They knew the gospel could not be stopped, and they turned the world upside down (see Acts 17:6).

I've met believers in countries like China and Cuba, where they have little freedom and much persecution. Yet the vibrancy of their faith and the dynamic spread of evangelistic impact is unstoppable. One Chinese leader explained, "Christians in China are praying for our Christian brothers and sisters in America. We believe we are handling our persecution better than you are handling your prosperity."[11]

WHAT?

I believe we also must evaluate *what* we are seeking in revival. It's been said that there is a difference between seeking revival from God and seeking God for revival. One approach pursues the result, the other is passionate for the Source. We would be wise to stop expecting certain prescribed outcomes and start embracing the filling of the Holy Spirit, with absolute surrender to His agenda of Christ's glory.

Over my decades of prayer leadership the Lord has burned into my heart that the only enduring motive for prayer is that God is worthy to be sought. As Martin Lloyd-Jones affirmed, "The inevitable and constant preliminary to revival has always been a thirst for God, a living thirst for a knowledge of the living God."[12]

HOW?

We also need an adjustment in *how* we are seeking revival. It seems like every day I hear of a new parachurch ministry with an impressive ambition to create a revival "movement." There is no doubt that many of these initiatives are absolutely sincere. In many ways, I am grateful for their emphasis and love the many godly saints who lead them. Lloyd-Jones said it well: "Believe me friends, when the next revival comes, it will come as a surprise to everybody, and especially to those who have been trying to organize it. No revival that the church has ever known has ever been an official movement."[13]

For many years, I focused passionately on the "fruits" of revival. But in recent days, I am thinking much more about the "roots" of revival. There are no fruits without roots. I believe that root system is connected to the unwavering conviction of praying people supporting praying pastors who lead praying churches that humbly rely on and earnestly obey the indwelling Holy Spirit for supernatural gospel impact.

A CONTAGIOUS SPREAD OF THE GOSPEL

We know and must believe that revival will result in an astonishing impact on the lost. We noted in chapter 1 from Acts 6:1–7 that the spiritually contagious environment of the early church, led by the prayer-focused apostles, supported by available saints, overflowed to extraordinary conversions, even among the Jewish leaders (remember, 6:3 + 6:4 = 6:7).

During the revival of 1857–58 that occurred through a movement of prayer begun by a Christian layman in New

York City (and during a national financial crisis), one million people were reported to become Christ-followers out of a population of thirty million.[14] That would be tantamount to 10.5 million conversions among the current US population. Professor Ed Hindson observes, "Revival among the saved will always result in an outburst of evangelism among the lost. Evangelism is the automatic byproduct of revival. One may prod an unrevived congregation to soul-winning activity with gifts and gimmicks, but such prodding is unnecessary in the revived church."[15] J. I. Packer underscores this: "God revives his church and then the new life overflows from the church for the conversion of outsiders and the renovation of society."[16] As we see in the book of Acts, "For we cannot but speak of what we have seen and heard" (4:20). They had seen the living, glorious Jesus and were hearing the voice of the empowering Spirit of truth.

Jonathan Edwards was perhaps the primary voice in the First Great Awakening in America during the eighteenth century. He noted that at the beginning, a few sermons were preached and some missions efforts were initiated, but a small number of converts were seen. "But then," Edwards notes, "God in so remarkable a manner took the work into his own hands and did as much in a day or two that, under normal circumstances took the entire Christian community, using every means at their disposal, with the blessing of God, more than a year to accomplish."[17]

May He unite our hearts in prayer. Oh God, take our work into Your hands. Eclipse our ordinary approach to life, family, and ministry with a fresh display of your extraordinary grace and power. And may we see it in our lifetime.

ROOF OFF, WALLS DOWN

Norman Grubb describes the contagious work of the Spirit so clearly. He notes that all Christian relationships are both vertical and horizontal. He proposes that revival incorporates continued two-way brokenness. Vertically, we must be careful to keep "the roof off between ourselves and God through repentance and faith."[18] Horizontally, we must also let the walls come down between ourselves and others. These walls of pride, self-esteem and self-respect must be levelled by transparent confession of broken relationships, harbored sin, and pretending to be better than we are. James 5:16, perhaps one of the least-practiced passages in the New Testament, states, "Therefore, confess your sins to one another and pray for one another, that you may be healed. The prayer of a righteous person has great power as it is working." Oh how we need to experience the power of this kind of honesty, confession, and believing prayer for one another. In revival, Spirit-filled Christians testify to one another about the great work of Jesus in their lives. They walk in the light as He is in the light. Roof off. Walls down. Continuous revival.

D. Martyn Lloyd-Jones has written, "Read the story of any revival that has ever taken place and you will find that the beginning of it is always the same. One man, or sometimes a number of people, suddenly become alive to the true Christian life, and others begin to pay attention to them . . . that is why our condition as believers is so important."[19] Quoting Norman Grubb again,

Revival in its truest sense is an everyday affair right down with the reach of everyday life—to be experienced each day in our hearts, homes, churches and fields of service. When revival does burst forth in greater and more public ways, thank God! But meanwhile we should see to it that we are being ourselves constantly revived persons . . . which, of course, also means that others are getting revived in our own circles. By this means God can have channels of revival by the thousands in all the churches of the world!

Robert E. Coleman noted, "In as much as all of us were made to glorify God, revival simply fulfills his desire that we might know him in *the fullness of the Spirit* and declare his praise to the ends of the earth."[20] Knowing that the purpose of the Holy Spirit in our lives is to glorify Christ (see John 16:14), we can affirm the declaration from Stephen Olford, "Revival is not just an idea; still less is it mere emotion or excitement. Revival is ultimately Christ himself, seen, felt, heard, living, active, moving in and through His Body, the Church on earth."[21]

JESUS' FINAL WORD TO US

The early chapters of the book of Revelation picture the glorious risen Christ among seven churches. Perhaps the closest teaching on what we label as "revival" is captured in our Lord's messages to the seven churches. In summary, He calls five of the seven to repent of their sinfulness and straying. His final word to all seven was not to "pray for revival" but to "hear what the Spirit says to the churches" (Rev. 2:7, 11, 17, 29; 3:6, 13, 22). The living Christ still walks among His church, ready to bring us back to the fullness of His life. He commands us to know, hear, trust, obey, and fully surrender to the indwelling Spirit, according to His revealed Word. Jesus is ready to launch a gospel contagion. And He is willing to start it in you.

CONTINUED RENEWAL
IN EVERY CRISIS

So, as we conclude, let me challenge you to keep praying through a crisis. If you are not in one today, just wait. Another one may be around the corner. God knows when we may need a dramatic shake-up to wake up from our drifting and get redirected to the pathway to renewal. He knows that the toughest of times, regardless of how or why they occur, can promote vital root growth, causing us to feed more deeply from the sufficiency of His sanctifying grace.

Let us *determine* to embrace the *convictions* that are pure, biblical, and powerful. Conviction to pray desperately, from the pulpit and the pew, with full availability to God, and in hope of a supernatural advancement of the gospel.

Let us *devote* ourselves to pray faithfully in *community* so that we will experience the rich lessons, blessings, and answers that are uniquely ours when we pray together.

Let us *develop* a deeper *competency* so that each one of us can live by and lead in prayer as we align our approach obediently and biblically to the life-giving pattern commanded by Jesus.

Let us *dream* of powerful gospel *contagion* from and by the indwelling Spirit of God that we might shine His light in the darkness of this present day and see transformation come to our lives, families, communities, nation, and world.

100,000 AGENTS OF RENEWAL

Daniel Henderson

Early in my pastoral ministry, I was actively committed to seeing a "prayer movement" occur in the city where I pastored. I also joined various gatherings of national parachurch prayer leaders as they planned the next strategy to mobilize prayer across the continent. These were good things and I still support these sincere efforts.

But one day the Lord convicted me that if prayer wasn't palpable in my own church, I should reconsider my efforts to try to export it. This was a turning point in my focus as I began to devote my best efforts to developing a dynamic, biblical prayer culture in my own congregation. God worked powerfully in the coming years, and the principles I learned have formed the basis of the coaching I have been able to facilitate with hundreds of pastors in our online cohorts.[1]

I've learned that there is a difference between a church that prays and a praying church. Every church sponsors some activities of prayer but fewer have developed a dynamic culture of prayer. When churches describe their prayer efforts, they may include dynamic multiple prayer gatherings each week and consistent training that affects the majority of the church. Or it may simply be a small group of prayer-motivated intercessors that are seldom highlighted and exclusively represent the "prayer ministry" of the local church. So perhaps we need to give some clarity as to what a praying church really looks like.

I truly believe that if every pastor and church would give their best efforts to seeing their local body truly become a praying people, then an organic, grassroots, quiet but powerful work of renewal would become contagious across our society. It would spread without fanfare via a glorious, informal network of praying churches ushering in supernatural impact in communities across the land.

Os Guinness observes:

> Our much needed reformation today will not come when Christian leaders sit around a board table with yellow pads and outline their vision from "mission" to "measurable outcomes." Rather, it will come when men and women of God wrestle with God as Jacob wrestled with the angel—wrestling with God, with their consciences, with their times and with the state of the church in their times, until out of that intense wrestling comes an experience of God that is shattering and all-decisive, and the source of what may later once again be termed a reformation. "I will not let you go unless you bless me."[2]

EVERY CHURCH SPONSORS SOME ACTIVITIES OF PRAYER BUT FEWER HAVE DEVELOPED A DYNAMIC CULTURE OF PRAYER.

My friend Pastor Dee Duke says it well: "Power flows to commitment." I can't help but wonder what might happen if 100,000 of us resolutely pursued biblical renewal in our lives, families, and local churches through a united commitment to some core practices. What if we simply sought to live intentionally, obediently, and strategically in the context of each local church?

For clarity, I want to suggest three overall congregational commitments, plus five commitments for leaders and church members respectively:

Three Church-Wide Commitments (all)

1. We will subscribe to a basic evangelical theology (similar to the National Association of Evangelicals[3] but inclusive of our specific doctrinal distinctives)

2. We will faithfully teach the Bible, typically in an expository approach, with full confidence in its authority and sufficiency.

3. We will seek to pray always with a missional focus in mind, so that as God shares His heart with us, we will be motivated and empowered to engage in gospel witness personally, locally, and globally.

Five 6:4 Commitments (leadership)

1. We will regularly *communicate an exemplary passion* for the priority of prayer in both the leadership

rhythms and the personal and gathered prayer experiences of the congregation.

2. We will endeavor to establish a *scheduled* rhythm of prayer, ideally to include:

- *Weekly*: We will gather in a time of significant prayer within the leadership and mobilize a prayer team that meets to pray for each and every worship service.

- *Monthly*: We will gather the church for a significant experience of Scripture-fed, Spirit-led, worship-based prayer.

- *Quarterly*: We will gather the church for focused missional prayer: prayer walks, prayer for the city, the nations, missionaries, etc. We will also seek to meet with pastors of other churches for prayer for the city in which we live.

- *Annually*: We will gather with other pastors *and churches* of our community to pray for the city, the region, the nation, and their respective leaders.

3. We will put a system in place to ensure that the pastors and/or elders are prayed for regularly.

4. We will put a system in place to regularly offer training to equip as many as possible to become confident and competent in leading life-giving prayer in the home, small groups, and various ministries of the church.

5. We will ensure that small/community groups, ministry teams, and other specialized meetings will devote significant time to biblical, balanced prayer every time they gather.

Five 6:3 Commitments (congregants)

1. I will earnestly endeavor to live a Spirit-filled life through daily surrender and regular rhythms of spiritual health (Bible reading/study, prayer, memorization, etc.)

2. I will maintain a reputable Christian testimony that reflects the fruit of the Spirit, loving relationships, and financial integrity.

3. I will eagerly discover and consistently use my spiritual gifts in serving faithfully and fruitfully in my local church to enable the leaders to better focus on "prayer and the ministry of the word."

4. I will pray faithfully and strategically for congregational leaders via the avenues provided by my local church.

5. I will participate eagerly and consistently in the regular opportunities of corporate prayer in the church and other church sponsored prayer initiatives as a vital contributor to the prayer culture of the congregation.

What if scores of thousands of praying people, in the pulpit and the pew, gatherings in thousands of churches, pledged their hearts to the enabling of the Spirit to see these commitments come to fruition? Could 6:3 + 6:4 become 6:7?

In this environment of deepening commitment, we can find ultimate contentment. We are able to swim in an ocean of sufficient gospel grace that meets us at every point of need—be it spiritual, physical, emotional, or relational. In the midst of crisis, we are secured to a supernatural sufficiency that proves to be our ultimate source of encouragement and endurance.

Oh God, may it happen quietly, palpably, undeniably —and ultimately for the advancement of the gospel and the glory of Jesus alone.

THE ESSENTIAL PRIORITY OF PRAYING WITH YOUR SPOUSE

Dennis Henderson

Our twenty-eighth year of marriage was our twenty-seventh year in ministry. You would think that a pastor would have an exceptional prayer practice with his wife. We didn't. We prayed together, some. It was usually on the fly. For us it took an awakening. Let me put it more honestly. It took a train wreck. Ministry had pushed our marriage down the line of priorities. Billie had been getting the scraps of time and focus. The one who is my first disciple was not being tenderly led in spiritual things. That crash, twenty-seven years ago, began a slow process of learning to deeply and regularly pray together. Prayer saved our marriage and ministry.

We now begin our marriage counseling with troubled couples with this question "How is your prayer time together?" One hundred percent have responded that they do not pray together. I ask pastors the same question in our private conversations and over 80 percent give the same answer.

Why was it so hard for couples to establish a rhythm of intimate prayer? Schedules ranked high on the list. Like me, husbands left early for jobs and came home late and tired. It seemed like there just was not a slot in our day where we could drive a stake to pray.

Intimidation was another barrier. Physically strong husbands felt spiritually inferior when it came to prayer. Even I felt like Billie was the superior prayer person when we began. The list of hindrances could continue, but the greatest hindrance is the enemy who battles to destroy our marriages and the life God wants us to have.

It is said in the human psyche that one must understand the benefits to attempt anything challenging. Here are a few of the many benefits as I look back.

1. I discovered the joy of walking in obedience. My obedience in leading our prayer life has given me deep peace and satisfaction that I am loving God as I love my wife through prayer.

2. Praying together leads to vulnerability, humility, and dependence. As we grew in our prayer times, I found myself growing in being open and vulnerable. We found ourselves talking openly after prayer of the issues that normally I would not discuss. This brought us closer to each other and, most importantly, dependent upon God.

3. Prayer changed us. Together we sought God's direction, wisdom, and His face. We continued to grow in our dependence on Him, we grew in our confidence in Him. In the movie *Shawdowlands*, C. S. Lewis says, "I pray because I can't help myself. I pray because I'm helpless. I pray because the need flows out of me all the time, waking and sleeping. It doesn't change God. It changes me." I became an authentic leader.

4. Praying together strengthens the bonds of trust, security, and intimacy. Billie has never felt more secure than she does today. Twenty-seven years of growing in prayer had brought about our greatest moments of intimacy spiritually and physically, which cements our lives together as one flesh.

SOME SIMPLE IDEAS
TO HELP YOU GET STARTED

1. Set a time. It cannot be left up to "when you get time." You must set a time. Morning is our best time. Though I might have a 6:00 a.m. meeting, I will return home to pray with Billie at 8:00 a.m. Set your time.

2. Baby steps. Today, Billie and I will pray 25–45 minutes each time. As you get started, take small steps. Five minutes consistently will turn to 10 or 20 minutes. However, your goal is not how long you pray. It is how *often* you pray. Praying often turns into a habit that you will not want to miss.

3. Pray short prayers. Some call this conversation prayer. Even today, if Billie prays for a lengthy time,

I will drift. We pray interactive prayers, which keeps us focused.

4. Use the Bible to start prayer. We allow God to start our conversation through His Word. We call this Scripture-fed prayer. We use the Psalms as our starter. The Scripture begins our thankfulness, pulls out our complaints and fears, and brings us to moments of worship. Take a psalm, read it together, and respond in prayer with what you see about God in the psalm. What you read will guide your thankfulness, requests, and worship.

There is no more important activity in a marriage than prayer. A new house, car, gadget, clothes will not do for your marriage what prayer will do.

Dennis and Billie Henderson have been married 55 years. They have four children and nine grandchildren. Dennis has pastored five growing churches and taught in three colleges in his 54 years of ministry. As a couple they are still active in ministry serving at Fusion Bible Church in Durant, Oklahoma, where he was the founding pastor. He also serves at the Southwest Regional Director for The 6:4 Fellowship. Billie and Dennis have spoken to ministry couples in fifteen countries and maintain an active speaking schedule for pastors and wives.

THE REGULAR PRACTICE OF PRAYING IN THE HOME

Troy Keaton

When the COVID-19 pandemic hit our world, it forced us all back into our homes. Things we had not done at home very often, maybe ever, were suddenly a regular part of our lives. Homeschooling, the practice of a select few, became everyone's alma mater. Homework was no longer just an assignment for the kids but the new normal for parents. Home cooking hadn't been so widespread since the 1950s. Even weekend worship was experienced in the confines of the house.

One of the greatest benefits of this crisis, we all hoped, would be a significant increase of prayer in the home.

LEARNED FIRST AT HOME

Several years ago, my four-year-old nephew Jesse lost both of his eyes when he suffered from a form of cancer known as retinoblastoma. In a day, he went from being a toddler who could see normally to never seeing again.

One of the stories I remember my sister sharing from that experience was the therapy Jesse had to have for some fairly ordinary task. With no ability to see, He would need training for things that are most often picked up by observation. For some time, a therapist would come to their home and teach Jesse things that most children learned by watching their parents. For example, pouring milk from a jug is a task we all learned by watching someone else do it. The challenge for Jesse was if he never saw these things performed, he would always need someone to do them for him. Prayer, like pouring, is best learned at home by observation, and like Jesse, we may need some training.

A STARTING PLACE

It is a beautiful thing when a church realigns its priorities to include corporate prayer. However, when church leaders prioritize prayer they often experience apathy or even resistance from a large segment of churchgoers. Why is this? We might be asking people to perform a task they've never practiced. Like Jesse we may need to be intentional about acquiring this skill. If prayer is not active in the home, we are attempting to engage people in something they are unfamiliar or uncomfortable with.

ROOTED IN FAITH IN A POWERFUL GOD

Prayer in the home must be rooted in a strong faith in who God is and what He can do. As parents we must have a relationship with Jesus that is real and personal and we must create an atmosphere of prayer by introducing the truths about God from His Word. When we know personally, communicate scripturally, and rely completely on the God of the Bible, prayer becomes a natural outflow of our lives to our children and grandchildren.

I remember as a child riding to the grocery store with my mother and grandmother. My grandmother was a "prayer warrior" who had unsaved children. She began to express to my mother her belief that God would save all her children and that even some would enter the ministry. While this seemed far-fetched to a ten-year-old boy, my grandmother's fervency and tears came from her understanding of the power of God. Over the years, God has answered her prayers. Her example of faith and confidence in the promises of Scripture and her willingness to cry to God in front of her family influenced an impressionable young boy that day.

EXPRESSED IN PRACTICAL WAYS

In 1 Thessalonians 5, right in the middle of Paul's brief bullet point list of admonitions, we find the familiar and sometimes confusing verse, "Pray without ceasing" (v. 17).

We understand that Paul is talking about living in the attitude of prayer and dependence upon God. It is not a ritual. It is the reality of living in moment-by-moment reliance. It also an exhortation to weaving prayer into the fabric of our various relationships in life.

If prayer is going to be powerful in the home, it must be practical. To apply this verse requires practical prayer and can be expressed a thousand ways a day in the home. It happens when the sunrise produces conversation and thanks to God. When a child's toothache is lifted spontaneously to the Lord. A blessing is received in the mail producing expressions of spontaneous worship to God. A college child worried about acceptance or finances and the family together waits on God's provision. Every day we are given opportunities to teach practical worship and reliance upon God.

If there ever was a place "praying without ceasing" applies, it is certainly in the home.

SUSTAINED BY INTENTIONAL DISCIPLINES

While prayer in the home must be a continual attitude of reliance that is expressed spontaneously, if prayer will endure in the lives of our families we need to intentionally make it a part of our regular family rhythms.

Regular mealtime prayer teaches long-term thanksgiving for all that we have. Morning prayer establishes a God-first reality in our lives. Evening prayer introduces the peace of God that allows our kids to sleep well. Praying together regularly teaches our children the power of corporate prayer.

Patterns of prayer over the long haul engrave on the hearts and minds of our families truths about God and reveal our heart's desires for them. These may be simple and oftentimes done without great emotion, but they establish prayer as an integral part of our lives.

THE BENEFITS ARE BOTH IMMEDIATE AND FOR OUR FUTURE

What if the crises of our lives produced a rebirth of prayer in our homes? What are the short-term and long-term benefits of prayer coming back home? Immediately our churches would be filled with parishioners who are engaging in life-changing prayer.

This reality would undoubtedly produce a fresh sense of renewal. The benefit would also be long-term. As we raise up a new generation of young people who have experienced for themselves the power of prayer, they will in turn pass on genuine spiritual life to generations to come. Oh Lord, let it be!

Troy Keaton is the founder and senior pastor of EastLake Community Church at Smith Mountain Lake, Virginia, overseeing a campus of over 200 acres that encompasses the church, a growing Christian school, and a soon-to-be-built retreat center for church leaders. He is a frequent conference speaker and a National Resource Leader for The 6:4 Fellowship. He and his wife Janel are parents of four children and enjoy time with their three grandchildren.

NOTES

Introduction: The Crossroads of Your Crisis

1. *Xinhua Zidian,* 10th rev., large-print ed. (Beijing: Commercial Press, 2004), 205, cited in "Chinese word for 'crisis,'" Wikipedia, last edited on April 27, 2020, https://en.wikipedia.org/wiki/Chinese_word_for_%22crisis%22.
2. Nora Naughton, Matt Wirz, and Cara Lombardo, "Hertz Was Already in Terrible Shape. The Pandemic Finished It Off.," *Wall Street Journal,* May 25, 2020, https://www.wsj.com/articles/hertz-was-already-in-terrible-shape-the-pandemic-finished-it-off-11590434631.

Step One: Decide to Let God Birth Fresh CONVICTION

Epigraph 1: G. K. Chesterton, *The Everlasting Man* (Garden City, NY: Image Books, 1955), 260.

Epigraph 2: Jim Cymbala, "How to Light the Fire," *Christianity Today,* May 19, 2004, https://www.christianitytoday.com/pastors/leadership-books/preachingworship/lclead01-22.html.

1. Adapted from the Introduction of *Old Paths, New Power: Awakening Your Church through Prayer and the Ministry of the Word* by Daniel Henderson (Chicago: Moody Publishers, 2016).
2. John F. MacArthur, *The MacArthur Study Bible* (Nashville: Thomas Nelson, 2006), 1610.

3. See the historical accounts offered by J. Edwin Orr in https://jedwinorr .com/resources/articles/prayandrevival.pdf, where he notes, for example, that just prior to the spiritual awakenings in the late 1700s, the Chief Justice of the United States, John Marshall, wrote to the Bishop of Virginia, James Madison, that the church "was too far gone ever to be redeemed." Voltaire averred and Tom Paine echoed, "Christianity will be forgotten in thirty years."

4. Os Guinness, *Renaissance: The Power of the Gospel However Dark the Times* (Downers Grove, IL: InterVarsity, 2014), 132.

5. John Baillie, *A Diary of Private Prayer* (New York: Scribner, 1977), 79.

6. Keeney Dickenson,"Prayer Life vs. Life of Prayer," Strategic Renewal, June 5, 2014, https://www.strategicrenewal.com/2014/06/05/prayer-life-vs-life-of-prayer/, adapted from *In Season and Out of Season* by Keeney Dickenson. Bold and italicized in original.

7. D. A. Carson, *A Call to Spiritual Reformation: Priorities from Paul and His Prayers* (Grand Rapids: Baker Academic, 1992), 35.

8. The Acts 6 narrative is what we call a "descriptive" passage. All descriptive passages are best interpreted by "prescriptive" biblical texts. Descriptive Scriptures tell about what did happen in the biblical account. Prescriptive passages teach about what should happen in biblical living. The Bible is full of clear instruction on the priorities of prayer, the word, the responsibilities of Christians to actively maximize their spiritual gifts in ministry, and the ultimate outcome of supernatural gospel influence in the world.

Step Two: Devote Yourself to a Consistent Experience of Praying in COMMUNITY

Epigraph 1: C. H. Spurgeon, *The Metropolitan Tabernacle Pulpit*, vol. 19 (London: Passmore & Alabaster, 1873), 218.

Epigraph 2: Quoted by J. Edwin Orr, "Prayer and Revival," in *Renewal Journal 1: Revival*, ed. Geoff Waugh, https://renewaljournal .files.wordpress.com/2014/12/rj-01-revival-pdf-147.pdf.

1. Adapted largely from Daniel Henderson, chapter 16, "Coming Out of the Prayer Closet," in *Transforming Prayer: How Everything Changes When You Seek God's Face* (Bloomington, MN: Bethany House Publishers, 2011).

2. Gene Getz, *Praying for One Another* (Wheaton, IL: Victor Books, 1982), 11.

3. Randy Frazee, *The Connecting Church* (Grand Rapids: Zondervan, 2001), 43.

4. Ibid., 85.

5. R. Albert Mohler Jr., "The Danger of 'I' in Christian Prayer," Albert Mohler.com, August 20, 2018, https://albertmohler.com/2018/08/20/danger-christian-prayer.

6. Michael Griffiths, *God's Forgetful Pilgrims* (London: Inter-Varsity Press, 1978), 24.

7. D. A. Carson, *A Call to Spiritual Reformation* (Grand Rapids: Baker, 1992), 35.

8. Daniel Henderson, "If I Were the Devil," Strategic Renewal, April 1, 2019, https://www.strategicrenewal.com/2019/04/01/if-i-were-the-devil/.

9. Joel Beeke, "Prayer Meetings and Revival in the Church," in *Giving Ourselves to Prayer: An Acts 6:4 Primer for Ministry*, comp. Dan R. Crawford (Terre Haute, IN: PrayerShop Publishing), 305.

10. C. H. Spurgeon, *Only a Prayer Meeting* (Ross-shire, Scotland: Christian Focus, 2000), 9.

11. Lewis O. Thompson, *The Prayer-Meeting and Its Improvement* (Chicago: W. G. Holmes, 1878), 16.

12. Jonathan Edwards, *An Humble Attempt to Promote Explicit Agreement and Visible Union of God's People in Extraordinary Prayer for the Revival of Religion and the Advancement of Christ's Kingdom on Earth, Pursuant to Scripture-Promises and Prophecies concerning the Last Time* (Boston: Printed for D. Henchman in Cornhil, 1747).

Step Three: Develop Your Biblical, Life-Giving Prayer COMPETENCY

Epigraph 1: Eugene Peterson, *Working the Angles* (Grand Rapids: Eerdmans, 1987), 44, 47.

Epigraph 2: D. A. Carson, *A Call to Spiritual Reformation: Priorities from Paul and His Prayers* (Grand Rapids: Baker Academic, 1992), 17.

1. This chapter is adapted largely from chapter 7, "How to Lead Life-Giving Prayer Experiences," in my book *Old Paths, New Power: Awakening Your Church through Prayer and the Ministry of the World* (Chicago: Moody Publishers, 2016)

2. Daniel Henderson, *PRAYzing! Creative Prayer Experiences from A to Z* (Colorado Springs: NavPress; 2007), 21

3. John Piper, "How to Pray for a Desolate Church," Desiring God Ministries, January 5, 1992, www.desiringgod.org

4. George Müller, *Autobiography of George Müller: A Million and a Half in Answer to Prayer* (Denton, TX: Wesminster Literature Resources, 2003), 153.

5. For information on our coaching, please visit https://www.strategicrenewal .com/coaching/.

6. A sample audio training session can be found at https://www .strategicrenewal.com/2014/08/10/leading-life-giving-prayer-times/ and a four-part DVD coaching resource is available at https://store .strategicrenewal.com/collections/video/products/how-to-experience-and-lead-life-giving-prayer-times-dvd

7. https://www.strategicrenewal.com/resources/?fwp_types=prayer-guide.

8. Cliff Boone, "I Never Feel More Like A Pastor Than When I Am. . . .," Strategic Renewal, April 22, 2015, https://www.strategicrenewal .com/2015/04/22/i-never-feel-more-like-a-pastor-than-when-i-am/.

Step Four: Determine You'll Become Spiritually CONTAGIOUS

1. Adapted from the conclusion of my book *Transforming Presence: How the Holy Spirit Changes Everything from the Inside-Out* (Chicago: Moody Publishers, 2018).

2. J. D. Greear, *Jesus, Continued . . . : Why the Spirit Inside You Is Better than Jesus Beside You* (Grand Rapids: Zondervan, 2014), 203.

3. https://www.merriam-webster.com/dictionary/contagion.

4. One common proof text is from Peter's sermon in Acts 3:19–20, where he exclaimed to the Jewish audience on the day of Pentecost, "Repent therefore, and turn back, that your sins may be blotted out, that times of refreshing may come from the presence of the Lord, and that he may send the Christ appointed for you, Jesus." Various interpretations

have been given for "times of refreshing from the presence of the Lord." Clearly, in context, this was a call to salvation to the lost Jews, not a teaching on revival for the church. Some view this as a reference to the future millennium. At best, it could be viewed as a description of the "cooling off that comes from blowing, like the refreshment of a cool breeze" (the literal meaning) that comes with salvation, along with the forgiveness and cleansing that Peter references in this evangelistic sermon. We might say that "the presence of the Lord" referenced here is always a source of "refreshing." If so, there must be the reality of the indwelling Holy Spirit, according the new covenant.

5. https://www.merriam-webster.com/dictionary/revived.

6. Bill Hull, *Revival That Reforms* (Grand Rapids: Fleming H. Revell, 1998), 17, 19.

7. Ibid., 19.

8. Norman Grubb, *Continuous Revival: The Secret of Victorious Living* (Fort Washington, PA: CLC Publications, 1952), 61.

9. Ibid., 80.

10. Grubb, *Continuous Revival*, 10.

11. Cited in Henry Blackaby and Claude King, *Fresh Encounter: Experiencing God in Revival and Spiritual Awakening* (Nashville: Broadman and Holman, 1996), 83.

12. Colin Hanson and John Woodbridge, *A God-Sized Vision: Revival Stories that Stretch and Stir* (Grand Rapids: Zondervan, 2010), 15.

13. D. Martyn Lloyd-Jones, *Revival* (Wheaton, IL: Crossway, 1987), 166.

14. Ronnie W. Floyd, "Pleading with Southern Baptists," SBC LIFE, December 1, 2014, http://www.sbclife.net/article/2329/pleading-with-southern-baptists.

15. Edward E. Hindson, *Glory in the Church: The Coming Revival!* (New York: Thomas Nelson, 1975), 21.

16. J. I. Packer, *Keep in Step with the Spirit* (Tarrytown, NY: Revel, 1984), 256.

17. Jonathan Edwards, quote in Collen Hansen, *A God-Sized Vision: Revival Stories That Stretch and Stir* (Grand Rapids: Zondervan, 2010), 179, revised in updated English.

18. Grubb, *Continuous Revival*, 18–21.

19. D. Martyn Lloyd Jones, *Spiritual Depression* (Grand Rapids: Eerdmans, 1965), 108.

20. Robert E. Coleman, cited in Walter C. Kaiser Jr., *Revive Us Again* (Nashville: Broadman and Holman, 1999), ix.

21. Stephen Olford, *Heart Cry for Revival: What Revivals Teach Us for Today* (Memphis, TN: Christian Focus, 2015), 94.

Appendix One: 100,000 Agents of Renewal

1. https://www.strategicrenewal.com/coaching/.

2. Os Guinness, *Renaissance: The Power of the Gospel However Dark the Times* (Downers Grove, IL: InterVarsity, 2014), 145–46.

3. https://www.nae.net/statement-of-faith/.

WHAT SEPARATES PASTORS WHO FINISH WELL FROM THOSE WHO DON'T?

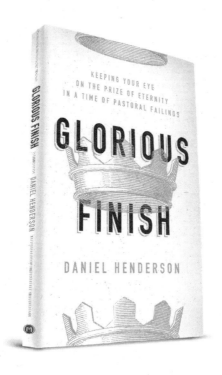

MOODY Publishers®

From the Word to Life®

When pastors fall to ruin, ministries get destroyed and congregants get wounded. *Glorious Finish* examines the roots of moral failings and how leaders can build habits to remain captivated by God's glory. For the sake of the Kingdom, learn how to serve with humility and integrity, keeping the end in mind.

978-0-8024-1943-9 | also available as eBook and audiobook

GET THE RESOURCES YOU NEED FOR WHEN LIFE TAKES AN UNEXPECTED TURN.

978-0-8024-2332-0

978-0-8024-2338-2

978-0-8024-2341-2

978-0-8024-2343-6

978-0-8024-2344-3

978-0-8024-2345-0

978-0-8024-2359-7

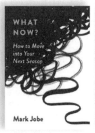

978-0-8024-2360-3

Be it in the midst of a natural disaster, global unrest, or an unforeseen pandemic, the repercussions of unprecedented change can leave us all reeling. Get the wisdom, encouragement, and peace you need to ease your anxieties, strengthen your relationships, and encounter the almighty God during such trying times.

also available as eBooks

MOODY
Publishers®

From the Word to Life®